Alex CRAWFORD
&
Phil H. LISTEMANN

Colour artwork: Malcolm Laird

Layout & project design: Phil Listemann

Copyright © Phil Listemann 2010
revised 2013

ISBN 978-29532544-5-7

All rights reserved. No parts of this publication may be reproduced, stored in a retrieval system or transmitted in any form or by any means, electronic, mechanical, photocopying, recording or otherwise, without permission in writing from the Authors.

ACKNOWLEDGEMENTS

Stefaan Bouwer, Chris Goss, Phil Jarrett, C.G. Jefford, SAAF Museum, Michael Schoeman, Andrew Thomas. Special thanks to Ken Smy for having providing the basic material regarding SAAF Furies.

Edited by Phil H. Listemann

philedition@wanadoo.fr

GLOSSARY OF TERMS

BOS : Board of Survey	RCAF : Royal Canadian Air Force
(CAN)/RAF : Canadian serving with the RAF	SAAF : South AfricanAir Force
F/L : Flight Lieutenant	(SA)/RAF : South African serving with the RAF
F/O : Flying Officer	Sgt : Sergeant
F/Sgt : Flight Sergeant	S/L : Squadron Leader
Lt : Lieutenant	SOC : Struck of charge
(NZ)/RAF : New Zealander serving with the RAF	Sqn : Squadron
P/O : Pilot Officer	W/C : Wing Commander
RAF : Royal Air Force	W/O : Warrant Officer
RAP : Reserve Aircraft Park	

INTRODUCTION

The Hawker Hornet, after it has been purchased by the RAF being allocated the serial J9682. The Hornet was basically the prototype of the Fury.

Without doubt the most attractive of all the pre-war biplane fighters was the Hawker Fury. Designed by Sydney Camm as a private venture, the Air Ministry had to take notice when the Fury proved to be the only aircraft capable of catching the Hawker Hart series of biplane two-seaters then entering service. The success of the Fury came from its engine. Developed at the same time the Rolls-Royce F.XIS proved to be a winner. Later renamed Kestrel, it went on to power most of Hawker's biplane aircraft until the advent of the monoplane fighters. These in turn were powered by the Kestrel's successor, the Merlin. The Fury's sleek shape came from its closely cowled inline Kestrel engine. Bracing and struts were kept to a minimum, which allowed it to break the 200 mph barrier.

Although superior to any other RAF fighter and able to catch the latest Hawker two-seat bombers, only small numbers of the Fury entered service. This may have been due to its relatively high price, although the RAF was committed to purchasing the Bulldog and no more funds were available from the Air Ministry. Sydney Camm's first inline engined fighter was the Hawker Hornbill, which first flew in 1925. As it failed to meet the Air Ministry's target speed of 200mph it was not accepted for production. Along with the development of the Hawker Hart, Sydney Camm also developed a lighter single seat fighter. Using Specification F.20/27 as a guide Hawkers went ahead and built a Mercury powered prototype as a private venture. The performance of this radial engined fighter proved quite conclusively that the future lay in in-line engines that could be streamlined into the fuselage. Incorporated into this design was the ability to change the engine to a Rolls-Royce FXIA, with little or no alteration to the basic shape of the fuselage. This would give an accurate comparison of the performance that could be achieved by radial and in-line engines.

This new fighter was named Hornet, and was displayed at the Olympia Aero Show in 1929 along with the Hart bomber. The fastest fighter of the day was the Bristol Bulldog, which had a top speed of 174 mph. When the first of the Harts entered service in 1929 they were faster than the Bulldogs by some 10-15 mph. This caused some concern in the Air Ministry, and they purchased the Hornet from Hawkers and re-named it Fury, although names like Flash, Flicker, Firebrand and Foil were also considered.

Initial trials were undertaken in March 1929 at Brooklands in the capable hands of Flight Lieutenant P.W.S. Bulman. The Hornet was later delivered to Martlesham Heath for service trials and wore the serial J9682. The performance of this new fighter was astonishing. With the 525 hp Kestrel IIS engine it was capable of a speed of 207 mph at 14,000 ft. It could climb to 10,000 ft in 4 minutes and 25 seconds. It was extremely light and responsive on the controls and had a fast rate of roll. As a result of these trials, Specification 13/20 was drafted around the design and an initial order for 21 aircraft was placed with Hawkers in August 1930 against contract 40559/30. The serials alloted were K1926 to K1946. The first flight of the first true Fury accured 7 seven months later, on 25 March 1931 at Brooklands and this first batch was deliivered the following month. This first contract was soon followed by another four, Contract 102468/31 for 48 Furies (Serials K2035-K2082) between January and April 1932, Contract 184986/32 for 16 (K2874-K2833 and K2899-K2904), all delivered in January 1933, Contract 252331/33 for 13 machines (K3730-K3742) delivered between September and November 1934 and finally 20 more against Contract 409396/35 (K5663-K5682) delivered in November and December 1935, making a total of 118 Furies built against the first five contracts. When an improved version of the Fury, the Fury Mk.II will appear later (to be seen in a future Allied Wings), these Furies will become Fury Mk.I. Due to the small number of machines taken on charge, only three front line squadrons were equipped with the Fury Mk.I.

The Fury was a composite construction of a steel tubular fuselage, tail assembly, wing spars and struts, with wooden wing ribs. The fuselage was rectangular in section and over this were applied decking stringers, which gave it the familiar oval shape. All steel tubes were cadmium coated and then stove enamelled. The fuselage was built up from four separate parts, which were then assembled together. The front section was the engine mounting. This had easily detachable aluminium cowling panels. The centre section contained the cockpit, machine guns, fuel and oil tanks. The fuel was housed in two tanks behind a fireproof bulkhead. Next came the rear section and finally the stern frame. The tail assembly was constructed the same way as the fuselage. The tailplane was adjustable for fore and aft trim by a wheel in the cockpit. This operated a screw-jack, which altered the incidence of the tailplane. The fin was offset to port by 3° to counteract the torque from the large two-blade propeller. The wings were of unequal span single bay type. Top and bottom wings differed in area, incidence, chord and dihedral. They were fabric covered apart from the leading edges, which were plywood skinned.

Armament consisted of two Vickers .303in machine guns, which were located in the top of the fuselage decking above the engine and gravity fuel tank. It was the basic armament for a fighter at that time. A total of 600 rounds were carried per gun. Firing levers were located on the control column spade grip. Power came from a Kestrel IIB engine, which was supercharged to give an output of 525 bhp at 14,000 ft. This drove a wooden two-blade fixed pitch wooden propeller.

Production line of the Fury in 1932 with a good view on the Kestrel engine. *(Phil Jarrett)*

Cuteway of the fuselage of a Fury. (*Phil Jarrett*)

TECHNICAL DATA
FURY MK.I

Manufacturer and production:
118 by H.G. Hawker Engineering Co.

Type:
Single-seat interceptor fighter.

Powerplant:
One 525 hp Rolls-Royce Kestrel IIS twelve-cylinder inline liquid-cooled engine.

Fuel & Oil
Fuel (Imp Gal):
Normal capacity : 50 [227 l]

Oil (Imp Gal):
4.5 [20.5 l]

Dimensions:
Span : 30 ft 0-in [9,14 m]
Length : 26 ft 8-in [8,17 m]
Height : 10 ft 2-in [3,10 m]
Wing area : 251.8 sq ft [23,4 m²]

Weights:
Empty : 2,623 lb [1 190 kg]
Loaded : 3,490 lb [1 583 kg]

Performance:
Max speed :
207 mph at 14,000 ft
[333 km/h at 4 250 m]

rate of climb : 2,225 ft/min [680 m/min]

Service ceiling : 28,000 ft [8 500 m]

Normal range : 305 miles [490 km]

Armament:
2 x 0.303-in [7.7 mm] Vickers II in the nose with 600 rpg.

Deliveries and Strenght
Fury Mk.I

Month (at last day)	Delivered	Total delivered	Op. Losses	Accident [1]	SOC	Available
April 31	21	21	-	-	-	21
.../...						
January 32	13	34	-	-	-	34
February 32	25	59	-	1	-	58
March 32	9	68	-	-	-	67
April 32	1	69	-	1	-	67
May 32	-	-	-	2	-	65
.../...						
August 32	-	-	-	-	1	64
September 32	-	-	-	1	-	63
.../...						
November 32	2	71	-	-	-	65
December 32	6	77	-	-	-	71
January 33	8	85	-	-	-	79
February 33	-	-	-	1	-	78
March 33	-	-	-	-	1	77
.../...						
October 33	-	-	-	-	1	76
.../...						
April 34	-	-	-	2	-	74
May 34	-	-	-	-	1	73
.../...						
July 34	-	-	-	-	1	72
.../...						
September 34	4	89	-	-	-	76
October 34	6	95	-	-	-	82
November 34	3	98	-	-	-	85
.../...						
February 35	-	-	-	-	1	84
March 35	-	-	-	-	1	83
.../...						
June 35	-	-	-	1	1	81
July 35	-	-	-	-	1	80
August 35	-	-	-	-	2	78
.../...						
November 35	15	113	-	-	-	93
December 35	5	118	-	-	-	98
January 36	-	-	-	1	1	96
February 36	-	-	-	-	1	95
.../...						
May 36	-	-	-	-	1	94
June 36	-	-	-	-	1	93
.../...						
August 36	-	-	-	2	-	91
September 36	-	-	-	1	1	89
October 36	-	-	-	3	-	86
.../...						
December 36	-	-	-	-	1	85
January 37	-	-	-	-	3	82
.../...						
March 37	-	-	-	1	2	79
April 37	-	-	-	1	2	76
May 37	-	-	-	2	1	71
June 37	-	-	-	1	-	72
.../...						
August 37	-	-	-	1	1	70
September 37	-	-	-	1	-	69
October 37	-	-	-	-	3	66
November 37	-	-	-	1	2	63

December 37	-	-	-	2	2	59
January 38	-	-	-	-	1	58
February 38	-	-	-	1	-	57
March 38	-	-	-	-	2	55
April 38	-	-	-	2	2	51
May 38	-	-	-	1	2	48
June 38	-	-	-	1	-	47
July 38	-	-	-	2	-	45
.../...						
September 38	-	-	-	-	2	43
.../...						
December 38	-	-	-	2	-	41
.../...						
February 39	-	-	-	-	1	40
.../...						
May 39	-	-	-	1	2	37
June 39	-	-	-	1	1	35
.../...						
September 39	-	-	-	1	-	34
October 39	-	-	-	1	-	33
.../...						
January 40	-	-	-	-	2	31
.../...						
March 40	-	-	-	-	1	30
April 40	-	-	-	-	2	28
.../...						
June 40	-	-	-	-	1	27
July 40	-	-	-	-	6	21
August 40	-	-	-	-	2	19
September 40	-	-	-	-	11	8
October 40	-	-	-	-	7	1
.../...						
July 41	-	-	-	-	1	-

[1] In case of accident, the month of the accident was selected above the struck of charge date (SOC).

The first Fury K1926 in flight while under testing at the A&AEE in 1931.

Fury M.Is of No.43 Squadron based at Tangmere, lined up at Mildenhall, 1 July 1935. *(IWM B(Arch) 128)*

No.43 Squadron
March 1931 - January 1939

The first unit to receive the Fury was No.43 Squadron based at Tangmere, under the command of Squadron Leader L.H. Slatter (later Air Marshall, Sir Leonard Slater CBE, CED, DSO, DFC). Deliveries began in April 1931 with K1942 and K1943 arriving on the 4th. The 15th saw the arrival of five more Furies, K1927-K1931, while a further nine, K1932, K1934-K1941, arrived on the 25th. By the end of the month a total of 18 Furies had been delivered. Straightaway the squadron proved what an exceptional aircraft the Fury was. Within a matter of weeks the squadron pilots were performing aerobatic displays with their new mounts.

In June three pilots, Flight Lieutenant E.T. Carpenter, Sergeants S.F. King and A.F. Underhill, took part in the Hendon Air Display. They put on a superb display of aerobatics and were praised for their skill and daring. At the Air Defence Exercises in July, No.43 Squadron achieved more successful interceptions than the rest of the squadrons put together. These air defence exercises were an annual event, although they were not flown in realistic settings. The targets were known in advance. It was forbidden to use cloud cover for tactical purposes. Only one fighter could attack a bomber at any one time. Bombers could not take evasive action. Pilots were not permitted to get closer than 100 yards to an 'enemy' aircraft. Despite these restrictions it was essential training for the young pilots who would later fight for real. The annual air firing camp was held at Sutton Bridge. Air-to-air and air-to-ground firing was practised. Target drogues were towed by ancient Bristol Fighters of WWI vintage.

The squadron's first accident and fatality occurred on the 28 February 1933. During a formation flying practise two Furies, K1933 and K1936, collided. The formation was at about 400 feet when the Furies came into contact. K1936 crashed into a ploughed field near Halnakar with the loss of Pilot Officer Robert V. Rolph. Pilot Officer Colin C. McMullen was able to land his damaged fighter. McMullen was slightly injured during the collision and was taken to the Royal West Sussex Hospital in Chichester. His Fury, K1933, was sent to Hawker for repairs but it is not sure that it was actually repaired because it was eventually converted to components two years later.

Later on 11 June a flight of three Furies took part in the International Air Meeting at Brussels. With falling rain and visibility at ½ a mile three Furies piloted by Flight Lieutenant John Hawtrey, Flying Officers Mermagen and Reynell, leapt into the air and put on a remarkable display of aerobatics, which pleased the crowd no end. The French squadron that was to follow No.43 Squadron called off their flight. After a slight improvement in the weather three Swiss Dewoitines went up but one of them hit a hanger roof and crashed.

There were many occasions when No.43 Squadron excelled them selves in the air in front of large crowds. When Portsmouth airport opened the squadron put on a magnificent show. A little later Flight Lieutenant T.N. McEvoy and Flying Officerf R.I.G. MacDougall put on a similar show over in Ireland for the opening of the airport at Newtonards.

In the summer of 1935 the Government directed that an experiment be carried out in which an RAF and a FAA squadron should exchange aircraft and perform each other's duties. It was thought that in the event of a war then both services would be able to exchange pilots as and when the need arose, without the need for further training. The Air Ministry selected No.43 Squadron, and they were informed that they would be converted to Nimrods, the naval equivalent of the Fury. The other half of this experiment was No.800 Squadron, FAA, who converted to the Fury. After a course of deck landing training the squadron was ready for its Nimrods.

At this time Mussolini invaded Abyssinia and the experiment was put on hold. A number of RAF squadrons were posted to the Middle East in case Mussolini had thoughts about invading Britain's Middle East possessions. As a result of pilots being posted out No.43 Squadron was put on cadre for several months. The squadron was run down so that at one point there were only half a dozen pilots on strength. That did not prevent another loss on 27 June 1935, K3742, when Pilot Officer N.D. Ashton was killed whilst performing aerobatics off Selsy Bil, Sussex. Fury K3742 had been taken of charge by the Squadron two weeks before, and was one of the twelve new Furies received in February and June 1935 to replace most of the ageing Furies of the first two contracts alloted to the Squadron four years earlier.

In early 1936 the squadron was slowly built up to full strength. By this time the Fury had been surpassed by the introduction of the Gloster Gauntlet. With the rapid expansion of the RAF pilots came and went, and the squadron spent most of its time practising formation flying, gunnery and interceptions and cross-crountries. It was during a such flight Pilot Officer G.E. Hollings was killed when his Fury, K1941, crashed into trees on the 30 October 1936. He was on his way to Sealand when he became lost in fog. While descending to a lower altitude he hit some trees on high ground near Hawarden, Cheshire. Despite intensive flying, the Squadron did not record only few write-offs. The following accident occured on 14 September 1937, when K1939 hit a fence on landing at Tangmere. The pilot was saved and the Fury was later declared as beyong economical repair.

The next loss and last for a Fury Mk.I was more dramatic and occurred on 4 April 1938. That day Sergeant Mathew Henry

A fine view of K1930. This clearly shows the black checkers marking devoid of the white segments. The white was added at a later date. *(Phil Jarrett)*

Baxter was up practising aerobatics when his Fury, K2074, broke up in the air and crashed near Roands Castle, Hampshire. Although Sergeant Baxter baled out he was too low and was killed. The Fury's swansong was at the Gatwick Air Display later in the year. Pilots from Germany, France and the USA praised the No.43 Squadron pilots for their magnificent display in spite of the unfavourable conditions. When the Fury Mk.II became available, the Squadron was partially equipped but continued to use a handful of Fury Mk.I until new equipment arrives, half a dozen being still on charge when the Squadron received the Hawker Hurricane in 1938.

Its last six Furies were finally transferred to Kemble in February 1939.

Three Furies of No.25 Squadron lined-up during summer 1932, K2059, K2055 and K2060. K2059 with its blue fin belongs to B Flight commander. K2055 will be involved in an accident a couple of weeks later, colliding with K2057, the latter being lost. *(Phil Jarrett)*

No.25 Squadron
February 1932 - November 1936

In December 1931 the second Fury squadron was formed. This was No.25 Squadron, based at Hawkinge and commanded by Squadron Leader W.E.G. Bryant. The first aircraft started to arrive on 10 February 1932 with K2061 and K2062. K2052 and K2054 arrived on the 20th, with K2055 and K2060 being received on the 24th. Other Furies, K2068 and K2070-K2072, arrived the next day. It seems that K2054 had a very short career with No.25 Squadron as it is believed that it was this aircraft, flown by Sergeant R.M. Ross, which was victim of the very first accident. Ross had been sent to collect a Fury at Hawker works when he decided to make some aerobatics to celebrate his arrival with the new mount. The experience ended in a upside-down landing. It is not sure that the aircraft was repaired as it was struck of charge on 28 July that year.

This accident won't be the only one and the following occured during the summer 1933. On 17 September, two Furies, K2055 and K2057, collided during formation practise. The latter aircraft flown by Flying Officer F.P.R. Dunworth, was abandoned and crashed near Hawkinge. while, K2055, flown by Flying Officer Arthur E. Clouston, a New Zealander, was able to land safely. This pilot will later know a sucessul career during the war, being awarded the DSO, DFC, and AFC and Bar and will retired as Air Commodore in 1960.

At Hendon in 1933 No.25 Squadron performed tied-together aerobatics. Led by Squadron Leader A L Paxton nine Furies took off all tied together. The highlight of their routine was a nine aircraft formation roll while still tied together! The aircraft then broke up into flights of three, still tied together, and performed a series of aerobatics. This was finished off with a 'Prince of Wales Feathers' break with one flight pulling up and looping after a vertical climb with the other two flights breaking off to port and starboard.

On the 7 August 1933 six Furies of No.25 Squadron were reported lost when a Hawker Horsley of No.504 Squadron crashed into a hanger. The Horsley was one of a formation of nine aircraft, which were carrying out formation flying. Three of the Horsleys broke formation and came in to land. As they were coming in over the hangers they were caught by a sudden gust of wind. One of the Horsleys, piloted by Flight Lieutenant F.W. Hartridge, hit a disused building with his right wing, causing the Horsley to hit the adjoining hanger. Escaping petrol from the Horsley poured onto the roof, which was very hot from the sun and burst into flames. Flight Lieutenant Hartridge and his observer, AC N.O. Connett, barely got out of the aircraft before it was a mass of flames. Inside the hanger six Blakcburn Darts which had been put into storage in the hangar and were mistaken for Furies by the local newspaper. Some confusion follow and the Air Ministry thought at first the aircraft which had burned were six Hawker Furies and a new contract for six remplacement Furies was prepared just to be cancelled when the mistake was discovered...the RAF was close to have six more Furies in its inventory. But it is interesting to notice that the RAF has been easliy hoaxed by its own press!

If No.25 Squadron did lose any Fury that day, the Squadron

Fury K2081 with K2080 were taken on charge in March 1933 by No.43 Squadron to replace K1933 and K1936 which collided the previous month. K2081 is seen here shortly after its arrival at Tangmere.
(Phil Jarrett)

Line-up of Furies of No.1 Squadron in 1934 with K2051 in front and K2881 just behind. The squadron emblem is clearly visible on the fin as well the serial painted on the underwings. (*Phil Jarrett*)

was less fortunate the following month when K2073 crashed at Thorney Island on the 25th. Despite intensive flying the Squadron lost only one more Fury Mk.I before receiving Fury Mk.II in October 1936. Shortly before the arrival of the Fury Mk.II, K2079, flown by Flying Officer F.G. Frow forcelanded in fog near Canterbury, Kent. If the pilots escaped major injuries, the aircraft was so badly damaged that it was struck off charge on 1 October 1936. In all, No.25 Squadron used 32 Fury Mk.I during over a period of 4 years and a half. Only four aircraft were wrecked, and no pilot killed, a pretty good record.

No.1 Squadron
February 1932 - November 1938

At Tangmere No.1 Squadron received its Furies in January 1932. The Squadron was led by a World War One fighter veteran, Squadron Leader Charles B.S. Spackman who had been awarded a DFC in 1918 and a Bar to it in 1922 for subsequent actions in Iraq in 1920 and 1921. On the 21st five Furies, K2035-K2038 and K2044, were delivered. Four days later on the 25th a further eight fighters, K2039-K2043 and K2045-K2047, were delivered. K2048-K2051, K2065, K2067 and K2069 were delivered in February bringing the squadron up to full strength.

Intensive training was carried out the following with and inevitably some accident occured. In April three of the Furies collided during fighter attack and formation aerobatics. The three Furies, K2035, K2038 and K2044, all carried out forced landings. Two of the aircraft were repaired, but K2038 was deemed beyond repair and struck off charge the following month. A few days later, a further collision occurred with the death of one of the pilots. Three Furies were carrying out a reconnaissance over Shoreham at 0930hrs when two of them touched. Flying Officer G.J.S. Chatterton was able to bale out of K2036, but Pilot Officer N.H. Jackson's parachute became entangled in his spinning aircraft, K2064, and he was killed in the resulting crash. Pilot Officer Jackson became the first pilot to be killed flying an Hawker Fury. The year 1933 was free of major accident, and in November, Squadron Leader Roy W. Chappell was appointed the new CO. Native of South Africa, Chappell was a very experienced pilot and as for Spackman, fought during the Great War as a fighter pilot and later in Iraq. In 1934, K2044 was involved in another collision on 23 April 1934. That day during flight formation attacks it collided with K2047 over Northolt, killing both pilots, Flight Lieutenant R. Brown and Flying Officer W.E.S. Tanner. Flight Lieutenant Brown had attempted to bale out but struck the ground before his parachute had time to open.

In May 1934 a decision was taken to send a flight of Furies to Toronto, Canada to take part in the Centenary Celebrations that were to he held in July. Five Furies would be shipped out under the command of Wing Commander G.C. Pirie, the Commanding Officer of Tangmere. The other flight members were Flight Lieutenant E.G.H. Russell-Stracey, Flying Officers G.J.S. Chatterton and J.W. Donaldson and Pilot Officer F.H. Dixon.

The five officers and twelve other ranks set sail for Canada on

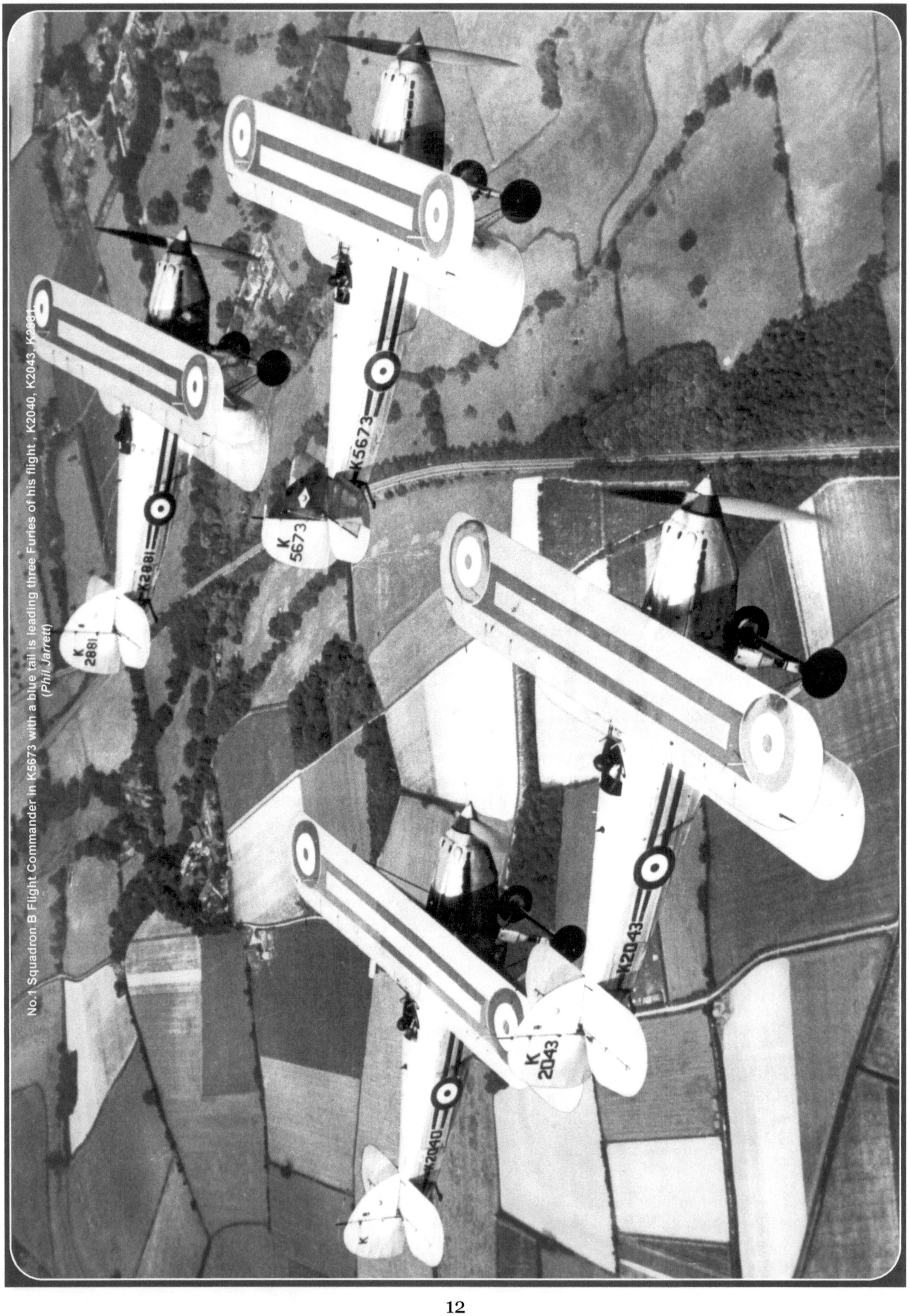

No.1 Squadron B Flight Commander in K5673 with a blue tail is leading three Furies of his flight, K2040, K2043, K2881. *(Phil Jarrett)*

9 June on board the SS *Alaunia*. The Furies were embarked on board the SS *Manchester Producer*. The Flight arrived at Montreal on the 19th and the Furies were sent to St Hubert, Quebec, for assembly.

After the celebrations, which took place on the 1st, 2nd and 3rd of July, the Flight embarked on a tour of nearby towns, where a number of displays were given. On 14 July the Furies were at Rockcliffe to take part in the Air Force Day. All five Furies were at Rockcliffe but only three took part in the flying display. The Flight set sail for the UK at the end of July. In October, Squadron Leader Cedric W. Hill assumed command of No.1 Squadron. When he was detached to a staff post in January 1936, he was replaced by Flight Lieutenant Theodre McEvoy from No.43 Squadron, another Fury squadron. Squadron Leader Hill returned at the Squadron in December 1936 before to be reaplaced by Squadron Leader F.R.D. Swain. Meanwhile, the Squadron life was pretty uneventful except when, on 20 July 1936, Pilot Officer H.H. Peel, a freshly rating pilot, overturned Fury K2045 after a forcelanding. Pilot Offier Peel was flying pretty low at 900 feet in rain and a very low ceiling when rpms of the engine began to drop. The engine stopped eventually at 100 feet. The aircraft was salvaged and sent to Hawkers facilities, but the aircraft was never repaired.

In March 1937 'B' Flight was disbanded and used to form No.72 Squadron, flying the newly introduced Gloster Gladiator. The Furies from 'B' Flight were sent to the newly formed 87 Squadron, including K2052, K2062 and K2878. The Flight reformed in April with three Furies.

For the 1937 Hendon Air Display 'A' Flight was chosen to perform for the squadron. The pilots that were chosen to display were Flight Lieutenant E.M. 'Teddy' Donaldson, Flying Officers 'Top' Boxer and 'Prosser' Hanks and Pilot Officer Johnny Walker. Flight Lieutenant Donaldson suggested that instead of the normal formation flying they should change positions during the display. They practised this and were soon looping and rolling four aircraft in a box formation. They would then changed to line astern and echelon formation. Their display was a great success and they were presented to the King after the show. On 29 May, the Squadron lost a pilot, Sergeant John Tanfield who was killed when his Fury, K2076, stalled and crashed into the ground at Tangmere.

At the International Air Meeting held at Zurich in August the flight was chosen to represent the RAF. The Furies were flown to Zurich via Hawkinge, Le Bourget and Dijon in France. The Tangmere Station Commander, Wing Commander Cedric Hill, and Pilot Officer A.C. Saunders flew two reserve Furies. The flight put on three displays in front of huge crowds. During the last day the conditions were not favourable for flying but Flight Lieutenant Donaldson and his pilots had practised in all weathers and they put on such a display that they drew tremendous applause from the crowds. Even a crack team of Italian Fiat CR32s couldn't compare to the Fury's display, which even brought congratulations from the Luftwaffe's General Milch. Known Furies taking part were K2043, K2089, K2881 and K5673 (Donaldson). In the last four months of 1937, the Squadron knew ver bad days. All started on 23 September with the loss of K2043 which was hit by K5675 after landing at Tangmere. K2043 became an instructional airframe in December. On 2 November, Sergeant C.G.T. Tucker saw his undercarriage of K2039 collapse on landing after it had hit the ground after a dive few minutes earlier. K2039 was declared being beyong economical repairs. Less than two weeks later, it was the turn of K2900 to be badly damaged. Sergeant Tucker was flying this Fury too, and hit a ridge whilst landing at Tangmere and once again the undercarriage collasped. The Fury was never repaired. Having lost three Furies in a couple of weeks, No.1 Squadron received five

Line-up of Furies of No.1 Squadron in 1935. K2900 is coded "K" and behind is K2901 coded "M". It seems that the invidual letters appeared around that time.

After having served with No.25 Squadron, K2878 was used by No.1 Squadron from 21 December 1936 until 15 March 1937. While serving with No.1 Squadron, it was flown by C Flight Commander with a yellow fin and wheels and was coded "L" painted in yellow just above the undercarriage. (*Chris Goss*)

Fury Mk.II on 10 December. Sadly for the Squdron, the black days were not over as one week later, on the 17th a number of Furies were in the air over Stanstead Park when two of them, K2901 and K2902, collided. Flight Lieutenant Harry Hamilton Peck and Sergeant Robert Edmund Patton both lost their lives. It was thought they either baled out or fell from their aircraft, and due to the low altitude their parachutes failed to open. In 1938, things did start better that 1937 ended. During a formation flight on the 22 February 1938 Pilot Officer M.V. Baxter left formation without permission. After losing height he struck some high voltage cables and crashed. The formation leader saw the flash as the aircraft hit the cables. Although the Fury did not catch fire Baxter was killed.

By that time, the Squadron were using mainly the Fury Mk.II, some Furies Mk.I remaining on charge until the arrival of the Hurricane in November 1938. In all, 41 Fury Mk.Is were used by No.1 Squadron and twelve were lost in accident killing 6 pilots. With those figures, No.1 Squadron is the Fury unit which knew the highest attrition rate.

By 1937, the RAF had begun its expansion and the Furies served to equip some squadrons mainly as an interim measure. Only one squadron was partially equipped with the Fury Mk.I, No.87 Squadron. It was formed on 15 March 1937 from elements of No.54 Squadron which was based at Tangmere. They received six Fury Is, K2052, K2062, K2066, K2878, K2882 and K2883, and thirteen Fury IIs. The Fury's stay was short lived as in June the squadron moved to Debden and began to re-equip with Gladiators.

Miscellaneous units

After being retired from front line duties the Furies found their way into a number of Flying Training Schools to be used for advanced pilot training. These were No.2 FTS (Digby and Brize Norton), No.3 FTS (South Cerney), No.5 FTS (Sealand), No.6 FTS (Netheravon), No.7 FTS (Peterborough), No.8 FTS (Montrose), No.9 FTS (Hullavington), No.10 FTS (Ternhill), and No.11 FTS (Shawbury). About 45 Furies Mk.I were used at a time or another by a Flying Training School, most finding their way to Nos.3 and 5 FTS. Advanced training was not an easy task, as 18 Furies Mk.I were wrecked but fortunately with a few casulaties as two pilots only were killed in these accident, both during gunnery practice. The first was Pilot Officer A.E.R. Ferris on 2 August 1937 in K5666 and the second was Pilot Officer C.W.E. Milburn who hit with his Fury K3730 ground target during gunnery pratic near Sutton

Fury K5677 whislt serving with RAFC in May 1937. It had served before with No.25 Squadron. The aircraft is partially painted in yellow. (*Andrew Thomas*)

Fury K5678 was delivered direct to the RAFC from the factory in December 1935 and spending four year at Cranwell. K5678 eventually knew another career with the SAAF. *(Phil Jarrett)*

The end of the road for K5679 of No.11 FTS, coded J. It hit target during gunnery training and lost a wheel, obliging the pilot to make a landing in very bad condition.

Aircraft Lost by Accident

Date	Unit	Pilot	SN	Origin	Serial	Fate
20.02.32	No.25 Sqn	Sgt Rainey M.H. Ross	RAF No.363698	RAF	K2054	-
05.04.32	No.1 Sqn	Sgt Sydney W. Bannister	RAF No.363845	RAF	K2038	-
26.05.32	No.1 Sqn	F/O George J.S. Chatterton	RAF No.29086	RAF	K2036	-
	No.1 Sqn	P/O Neville H. Jackson	RAF No?	RAF	K2064	†
17.09.32	No.25 Sqn	F/O Felix P.R. Dunnworth	RAF No.28185	RAF	K2057	-
28.02.33	No.43 Sqn	P/O Colin C. McMullen	RAF No.32118	RAF	K1933	-
	No.43 Sqn	P/O Robert V. Rolph	RAF No?	(CAN)/RAF	K1936	†
25.09.33	No.1 Sqn	Sgt William M. Hodge	RAF No.507233	RAF	K2073	†
23.04.34	No.1 Sqn	F/L Richard Brown	RAF No?	RAF	K2047	†
		F/O William E.S. Tanner	RAF No?	RAF	K2044	†
06.01.36	No.6 FTS	P/O Dennis V.W. Francis	RAF No.37165	RAF	K3737	-
27.06.35	No.43 Sqn	P/O Norman D. Ashton	RAF No?	RAF	K3742	†
04.02.36	No.2 FTS	P/O Peter J.G. Davies	RAF No?	RAF	K3732	-
08.07.36	No.43 Sqn	P/O Frederick E. Rosier	RAF No.37425	RAF	K5671	-
20.07.36	No.1 Sqn	P/O Harry H. Peck	RAF No?	RAF	K2045	-
30.07.36	No.1 Sqn	P/O Alexander C. Rabagliati	RAF No.37209	RAF	K2067	-
03.09.36	No.25 Sqn	F/O Francis G. Frow	RAF No.36013	RAF	K2079	-
07.10.36	RAFC	F/L Roy J.O. Bartlett	RAF No?	RAF	K5682	†
	RAFC	Flt Cadet Howard F. Burton	RAF No.33227	RAF	K5681	-
30.10.36	No.43 Sqn	P/O George E. Hollings	RAF No?	RAF	K1941	†
18.03.37	No.11 FTS	LAC Frederick C. Thurgar	RAF No.580283	RAF	K5679	-
16.04.37	No.5 FTS	LAC John E. Proctor	RAF No.563641	RAF	K3734	-
26.05.37	No.43 Sqn	P/O Lucius J. Fry	RAF No.39229	RAF	K5668	-
29.05.37	No.1 Sqn	Sgt John G. Tanfield	RAF No.58004	RAF	K2076	†
28.06.37	No.11 FTS	P/O William H. Martyn	RAF No.39324	(CAN)/RAF	K1937	-
02.08.37	No.11 FTS	P/O Albert E.R. Ferris	RAF No?	RAF	K5666	†
14.09.37	No.43 Sqn	*No details available*	?		K1939	
23.09.37	No.1 Sqn	-	*ground collision*	-	K2043	-
02.11.37	No.1 Sqn	Sgt Cyril G.T. Tucker	RAF No.580216	RAF	K2039	-

Date	Unit	Pilot	Service No	Nationality	Serial	Fate
16.11.37	No.1 Sqn	Sgt Cyril G.T. Tucker	RAF No.580216	RAF	K2900	-
17.12.37	No.1 Sqn	Sgt Robert E. Patten	RAF No.562244	RAF	K2901	†
	No.1 Sqn	P/O Harry H. Peck	RAF No?	RAF	K2902	†
22.02.38	No.1 Sqn	P/O Merton V. Baxter	RAF No.37957	(NZ)/RAF	K2061	†
23.02.38	No.1 Sqn	*Ground accident*	-	-	K2881	-
01.03.38	No.11 FTS	P/O Richard P.Y. Cross	RAF No.40087	RAF	K2878	-
01.04.38	No.11 FTS	LAC Ian N. Macrae	RAF No.565633	RAF	K2883	-
04.04.38	No.43 Sqn	Sgt Matthew H. Baxter	RAF No.563858	RAF	K2074	†
20.06.38	No.2 FTS	P/O Colin W.E. Milburn	RAF No?	RAF	K3730	†
13.07.38	No.11 FTS	P/O Ruppert F. Smythe	RAF No.40436	(IRE)/RAF	K1938	-
29.07.38	No.3 FTS	P/O James R.B. Hartnoll	RAF No.70857	RAF	K2058	-
07.12.38	No.3 FTS	LAC William H. Dunwoodie	RAF No.53099	RAF	K5673	-
10.12.38	No.1 AAS	F/L Lionel W. Saben	RAF No.34178	RAF	K1940	-
17.03.39	No.5 FTS	Cpl Henry V. Hubbard	RAF No.565894	RAF	K3736	-
23.05.39	C.F.S.	P/O James H.S. Broughton	RAF No.40880	RAF	K2904	-
29.06.39	No.3 FTS	P/O William B. Wheelwright	RAF No.41763	RAF	K2035	-
06.09.39	No.6 FTS	P/O Keith J. Masters	RAF No.41941	RAF	K3738	-
29.06.40	No.9 MU	S/L George N. Warrington	RAF No.28101	RAF	K5664	-

Total: 48

Other early SOC dates and Ground Instructional Airframe

Serial	Date	Notes
K2049	10.08.32	Presumed damaged in an accident. No further detail.
K2072	10.08.32	Presumed damaged in an accident. Converted to components in August 1935.
K2068	09.03.33	Presumed damaged in an accident. No further detail.
K2056	08.05.34	Presumed damaged in an accident. No further detail.
K2053	28.03.35	Presumed damaged in an accident. Converted to components.
K1942	07.01.36	Believed time-expired. To 749M
K2037	27.05.36	Believed time-expired. To 849M
K1944	09.06.36	Believed time-expired. To 853M
K1943	20.01.37	Believed time-expired. To 974M
K2042	Feb-37	Believed time-expired. To 925M
K2069	15.03.37	Believed time-expired. To 946M
K2041	11.04.37	Believed time-expired. To 947M
K2078	15.04.37	Believed time-expired. To 948M
K1931	13.05.37	Believed time-expired. SOC
K2063	09.08.37	Believed time-expired. To 976M
K2065	04.10.37	Believed time-expired. To 992M
K1932	11.10.37	Believed time-expired. To 987M
K2075	20.10.37	Believed time-expired. To 998M
K2051	30.11.37	Believed time-expired. To 1017M
K2048	10.12.37	Believed time-expired. To 1018M
K2043	15.12.37	Believed time-expired. To 1019M
K2060	20.12.37	Believed time-expired. To 1026M
K1946	02.03.38	Time-expired. To 1045M
K2055	02.03.38	Time-expired. To 1044M
K2081	05.04.38	Believed time-expired. To 1048M
K2881	07.04.38	Ground accident. Not repaired. To 1049M
K2070	01.09.38	Time-expired. To 1112M
K2046	20.09.38	Time-expired. To 1131M
K3736	01.05.39	Time-expired. To 1464M
K2062	01.05.39	Time-expired. To 1465M
K2878	17.01.40	Time-expired. To 1719M
K5667	17.03.40	Time-expired. To 1723M
K2879	27.04.40	Time-expired. To 1911M
K2052	18.06.40	Time-expired. To 2018M
K2874	10.10.40	Time-expired. To 2239M
K2882	10.10.40	Time-expired. To 2241M
K5664	10.10.40	Time-expired. To 2246M
K2080	18.07.41	Time-expired. To 2639M

TIME OF OPERATIONAL USE
FLYING UNITS

SERIALS			DATE ON SQN	DATE OFF SQN
K1926:	1 Sqn		?	?
K1927:	43 Sqn		?	03.04.36
K1928:	43 Sqn		15.04.31	24.08.32

Fury K1928 while serving with No.43 Sqn during Winter 1931-1932. The fin and spinner are believed to be blue, the distinctive markings for the B Flight leader.

K1929:	43 Sqn	15.04.31	24.10.34
K1930:	43 Sqn	15.04.31	19.10.35
	25 Sqn	01.07.36	29.07.36
	43 Sqn	29.07.36	06.02.39
K1931:	43 Sqn	15.04.31	01.10.34
K1932:	43 Sqn	25.04.31	11.10.37
K1933:	43 Sqn	25.10.31	28.02.33

While Fury K1928 was the mount of the B Flight leader, K1933 became the mount of the A Flight with fin and spinner painted in red. K1933 was lost in an accident in February 1933 when it collided with K1936.

K1934:	43 Sqn	25.04.31	29.05.32
	43 Sqn	?	29.03.35

K1935:	43 Sqn	25.04.31	12.01.32
K1936:	43 Sqn	25.04.31	28.02.33
K1937:	43 Sqn	25.04.31	13.03.35

Left, Fury K1938 served during four years with No.43 Squadron, later with No.11 FTS where it was coded '2'.

Right, the same aircraft taken during engine warm-up. The wheels and the the individual number '2' are belived to be blue. The spinner is possible blue as well.

K1938:	43 Sqn	25.04.31	06.04.35
K1939:	43 Sqn	25.04.31	28.09.31
		?	14.09.37
K1940:	43 Sqn	25.04.41	23.03.32
	1 Sqn	02.11.32	?
K1941:	43 Sqn	25.04.31	04.11.36
K1942:	43 Sqn	04.04.31	07.01.36

Fury K1942 while serving with No.43 Squadron. The lack of painted rudder suggests that the photo was taken after August 1934.

| K1943: | 43 Sqn | 04.04.31 | 20.01.37 |
| K1944: | 43 Sqn | 28.04.31 | 09.06.36 |

Fury K1944 served without major incident with No.43 Sqn until becoming an instructional airframe form June 1936 onwards, probably because it had reached its airframe limit.

K1945:	43 Sqn	24.04.31	?
	25 Sqn	?	04.07.35
K1946:	25 Sqn	01.07.36	28.07.36
	43 Sqn	28.07.36	02.03.38

Fury K1946 was on No.43 Squadron charge from July 1936 onwards. Nevertheless, it is obvious that this Fury did not receive new paint since the factory as the fuselage roundel is clearly faded out and the rudder is still painted, offically removed after August 1934! (*Andrew Thomas*)

K2035:	1 Sqn	21.01.32	?
	43 Sqn	?	?
K2036:	1 Sqn	21.01.32	26.05.32
K2037:	1 Sqn	21.01.32	27.05.36
K2038:	1 Sqn	21.01.32	05.04.32
K2039:	1 Sqn [D]	25.01.32	02.11.37
K2040:	1 Sqn	25.01.32	05.08.32

K2041:	1 Sqn	25.01.32	?
	25 Sqn	?	11.04.37

K2041 of No.1 Squadron in flight before August 1934. Note the wheel and spinner painted, probably in red, colour of the A Flight.

K2042:	1 Sqn [C]	25.01.32	?
K2043:	1 Sqn [B]	25.01.32	23.09.37
K2044:	1 Sqn [C]	21.01.32	05.04.32
K2045:	1 Sqn	25.01.32	20.07.36
K2046:	1 Sqn	25.01.32	20.09.38
K2047:	1 Sqn	25.01.32	23.04.34
K2048:	1 Sqn	10.02.32	?
	25 Sqn	?	10.12.37

K2048 was No.1 Squadron's CO, Squadron Leader C.B.S Spackman. Later, K2048 served with No.25 Squadron.

K2048 still with No.1 Squadron has now new markings. Note that now the fin and tailplane are painted in black suggesting a Flight Commander's mount. Note that the wheels are not painted at all.

K2049:	1 Sqn	20.02.32	10.08.32
K2050:	1 Sqn	20.02.32	04.01.33
	43 Sqn	28.06.35	23.11.36
K2051:	1 Sqn	20.02.32	29.04.36
	43 Sqn	01.07.36	28.07.36
	25 Sqn	28.07.36	11.12.36
	1 Sqn	11.12.36	30.11.37
K2052:	25 Sqn	20.02.32	11.12.36
	1 Sqn	11.12.36	15.03.37
	87 Sqn	15.03.37	*June 37*
	43 Sqn	?	03.01.39
K2053:	25 Sqn	20.02.32	08.01.35
	43 Sqn	?	28.03.35
K2054:	25 Sqn	20.02.32	28.07.32
K2055:	25 Sqn	24.02.32	03.02.34
		17.05.34	11.12.36
	1 Sqn	11.12.36	02.03.38
K2056:	25 Sqn	24.02.32	08.05.34

Fury K2054 seen in February 1934 a couple of weeks before being struck off RAF charge. It flew all its career with No.25 Sqn.

K2057:	25 Sqn	24.02.32	17.09.32
K2058:	25 Sqn	24.02.32	31.01.33
K2059:	25 Sqn	24.02.32	30.03.36
K2060:	25 Sqn	24.02.32	?
	1 Sqn	?	20.12.37
K2061:	25 Sqn	10.02.32	?
	1 Sqn [B]	?	22.02.38
K2062:	25 Sqn	10.02.32	27.07.32
		04.06.34	27.01.37
	1 Sqn	27.01.37	15.03.37
	87 Sqn	15.03.37	?
K2063:	1 Sqn [C]	10.02.32	24.03.37
K2064:	1 Sqn	10.02.32	26.05.32
K2065:	1 Sqn [J]	10.02.32	04.12.34
K2066:	1 Sqn [K]	04.06.32	?
	25 Sqn	?	15.03.37
	87 Sqn	15.03.37	*June 37*
K2067:	1 Sqn [I]	25.02.32	?
	25 Sqn	?	?
K2068:	25 Sqn	25.02.32	09.03.33

Fury K2061 No.1 Squadron starting up for another routine flight. Note the individual letter 'B' which was painted on each side of the bulkhead. This aircraft belongs to A Flight and has its wheels and propeller painted in red.
(Phil Jarrett)

K2065 of No.1 Squadron, coded 'J', painted in red on the engine cowling. The top fuselage, rudder, spinner and wheels are painted in yellow, colour of the C Flight. The fact that the top fuselage is painted in the Flight colour denotes the Flight Commander's aircraft.

K2070 was the personal mount of the Squadron's CO, Squadron Leader W.E.C. Bryant in 1932. Note the Squadron Leader pennant behind the cockpit. Wheels, fin and elevators are black.
(C.G. Jefford)

K2071 of No.25 Squadron, prior to August 1934. The fin, elevators and wheels are painted in blue, B Flight colour.

After having served with No.25 Squadron, K2071 later served with No.3 FTS. The insignia of this Flying Training School has been painted on the fin, identified with a number '3' in the middle.

K2078 served only with No.25 Squadron. Note the squadron insignia on the fin. It belongs to A Flight, with red spinner and wheels.

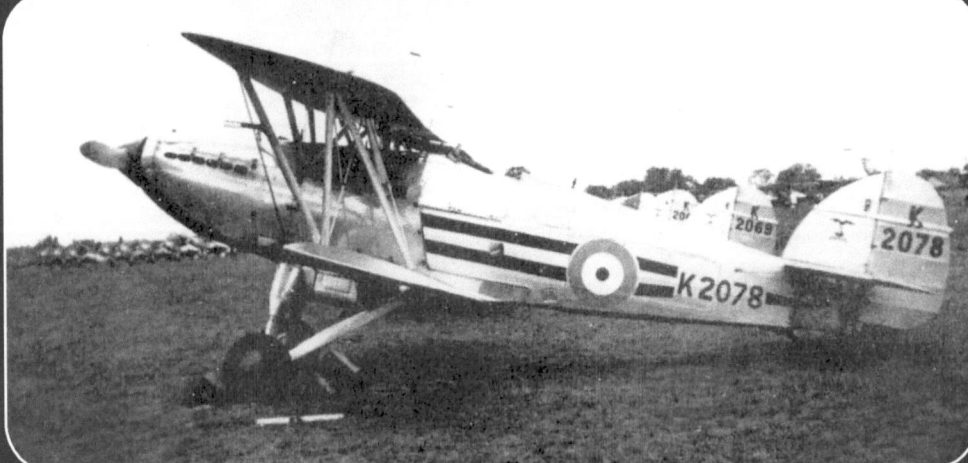

K2079 served also with No.25 Squadron only but there is no squadron emblem on the fin. It belongs to A Flight too, with red spinner and wheels. This photo is reported to have been taken during the summer 1936, shortly before it was destroyed in a crash.
(*Andrew Thomas*)

K2069:	1 Sqn	25.02.32	?
	25 Sqn	?	15.03.37
K2070:	25 Sqn	25.02.32	11.12.36
	43 Sqn	11.12.36	01.09.38
K2071:	25 Sqn	25.02.32	27.07.35
K2072:	25 Sqn	25.02.32	10.08.32
K2073:	25 Sqn	04.06.32	25.09.33
K2074:	1 Sqn [J]	24.10.32	?
	43 Sqn	?	04.04.38
K2075:	1 Sqn	17.01.33	01.07.36
	43 Sqn	01.07.36	20.10.37
K2076:	43 Sqn	17.01.33	19.10.35
		01.07.36	24.07.36
	25 Sqn	24.07.36	11.12.36
	1 Sqn [B]	11.12.36	29.05.37
K2077:	25 Sqn	05.08.32	12.03.34
K2078:	25 Sqn	12.01.33	15.04.37
K2079:	25 Sqn	31.03.33	03.09.36
K2080:	43 Sqn	14.03.33	03.01.39

Side view of K2080 with No.43 Sqn markings. It became an instructional airframe in July 1941 as 2639M.

K2081:	43 Sqn	14.03.33	05.04.38
K2082:	43 Sqn	16.12.33	03.02.34
K2874:	-		
K2875:	-		
K2876:	-		
K2877:	25 Sqn	03.11.32	04.01.34
K2878:	25 Sqn	29.11.33	21.12.36
	1 Sqn [L]	21.12.36	15.03.37
	87 Sqn	15.03.37	*June 37*
K2879:	-		
K2880:	-		
K2881:	1 Sqn	03.02.34	23.02.38
K2882:	25 Sqn	03.02.34	11.12.36
	43 Sqn	11.12.36	15.03.37
	87 Sqn	15.03.37	*June 37*
	43 Sqn	?	06.02.39
K2883:	25 Sqn	03.02.34	11.12.36
	43 Sqn	11.12.36	15.03.37
	87 Sqn	15.03.37	*June 37*
K2899:	1 Sqn [M]	03.02.34	?

Like many Hawker Furies, Fury K2883 was sent to Flying Training School as advanced trainer. Here K2883 is seen at No.11 FTS, on the ground at Wittering, attended by its pilot, Pilot Officer Derrick Fairbairn and his two mechanics, in 1937.

K2902 of No.1 Squadron. It belongs to B Flight with its fin, wheels and spinner painted in blue. Its individual letter 'A' can be noticed on the cowling, painted in red. No.1 Squadron seems to have been the only Fury squadron to have used individual letters.

K3731 of No.43 Squadron taxiing for another training flight. Note the fin and wheel and spinner painted in red for the A Flight.

Serial	Squadron	Date	Date
K2900:	1 Sqn [K]	28.05.34	19.10.35
		?	16.11.37
K2901:	1 Sqn	28.05.34	19.10.35
		?	17.12.37
K2902:	1 Sqn [A]	26.06.34	17.12.37
K2903:	1 Sqn	?	06.10.34
K2904:	-		
K3730:	43 Sqn	15.02.35	?
K3731:	43 Sqn	15.02.35	30.12.38
K3732:	-		
K3733:	43 Sqn	15.02.35	09.10.35
K3734:	43 Sqn	15.02.35	09.10.35
K3735:	43 Sqn	15.02.35	09.10.35
K3736:	43 Sqn	15.02.35	19.10.35
K3737:	43 Sqn	15.02.35	12.10.35
K3738:	43 Sqn	15.02.35	12.10.35
K3739:	43 Sqn	15.02.35	12.10.36
K3740:	43 Sqn	12.06.35	?
K3741:	43 Sqn	12.06.35	05.09.35
K3742:	43 Sqn	12.06.35	27.06.35
K5663:	-		
K5664:	-		
K5665:	-		
K5666:	-		
K5667:	-		
K5668:	-		
K5669:	-		
K5670:	-		
K5671:	43 Sqn	25.03.36	08.07.36
K5672:	25 Sqn	01.05.36	19.12.36
	43 Sqn	19.12.36	06.02.39
K5673:	1 Sqn	02.06.36	?
K5674:	43 Sqn	02.06.36	06.02.39
K5675:	43 Sqn	01.07.36	03.01.39
K5676:	-		
K5677:	25 Sqn	?	23.10.36
K5678:	-		
K5679:	-		
K5680:	-		
K5681:	-		
K5682:	-		

Line-up of Furies of No.43 Sqn. A mechanic is seated in K2074 and had started the engine to warm it up.

K5666 was delivered to RAFC on 25 February 1936 but was handed over to No.11 FTS two months later and coded '4'. It was destroyed in an accident the following year. *(Andrew Thomas)*

K5669 coded '9' at No.7 FTS in 1937. It never served with a front line squadron. Fin, wheel and spinner are believed to be light blue and the number 9 in white.

Shortly before WW2, aircraft of the FTS were repainted with trainer yellow to become more visible in flight. That suggests that K5670 was at that time flying with No.5 FTS. Note the wheels, spinner and the the number 3, which are believed to be in black and not red.

The No.1 Sqn's CO in K2041 leading eight other Hawker Fury Mk.Is in the early thirties.

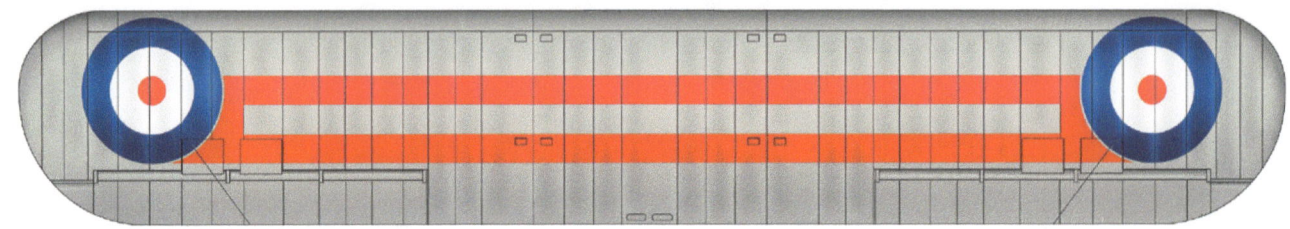

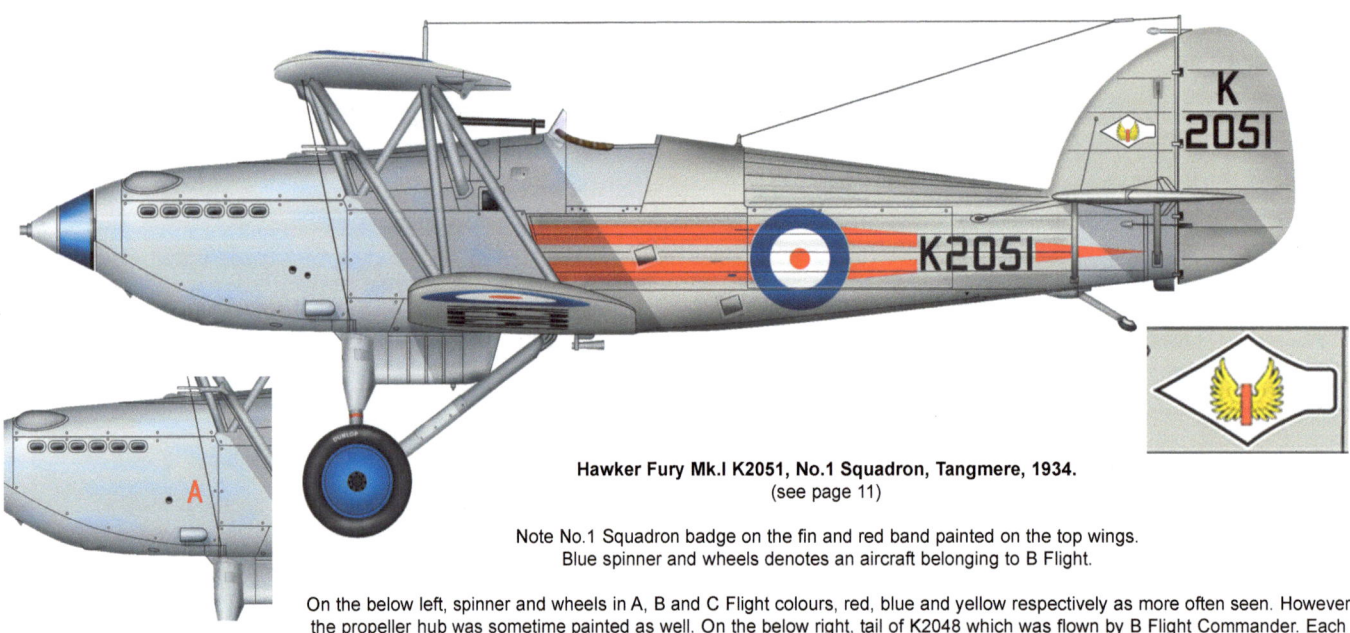

Hawker Fury Mk.I K2051, No.1 Squadron, Tangmere, 1934.
(see page 11)

Note No.1 Squadron badge on the fin and red band painted on the top wings.
Blue spinner and wheels denotes an aircraft belonging to B Flight.

On the below left, spinner and wheels in A, B and C Flight colours, red, blue and yellow respectively as more often seen. However the propeller hub was sometime painted as well. On the below right, tail of K2048 which was flown by B Flight Commander. Each Flight commander had the fin and tailplane painted in the colour of the Flight.

On the upper left : At a time, aircraft received an individual letter which was painted in red near the engine bulkhead.

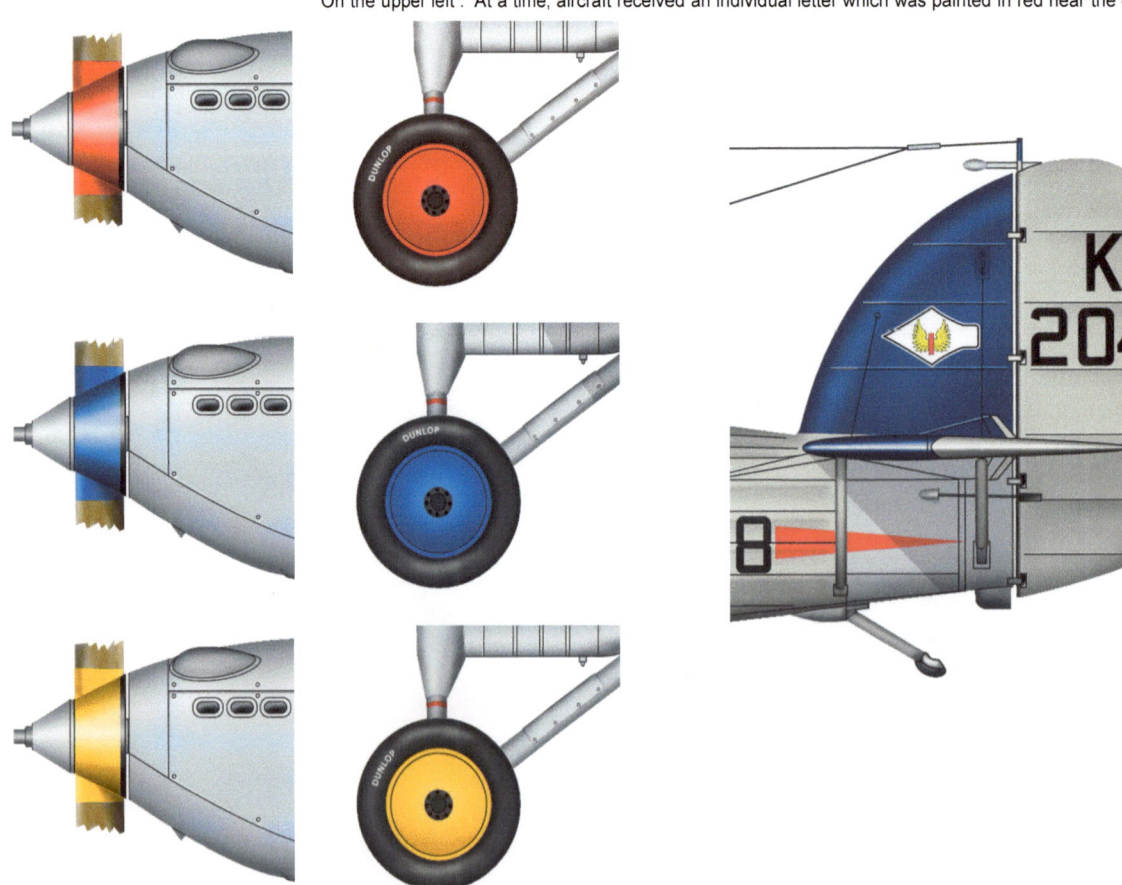

Hawker Fury Mk.I K2070, No.25 Squadron, Hawkinge, 1932.
(see p23)

K2070 was the personal mount of the Squadron's CO, Squadron Leader W.E.C. Bryant in 1932. Note the Squadron Leader pennant behind the cockpit. Wheels, fin and elevators are black.
K2070 is still wearing rudder stripng which were abandoned on 1 August 1934.
Note also the upper wings roundels covering control surfaces, roundels which were later reduced after August 1934.

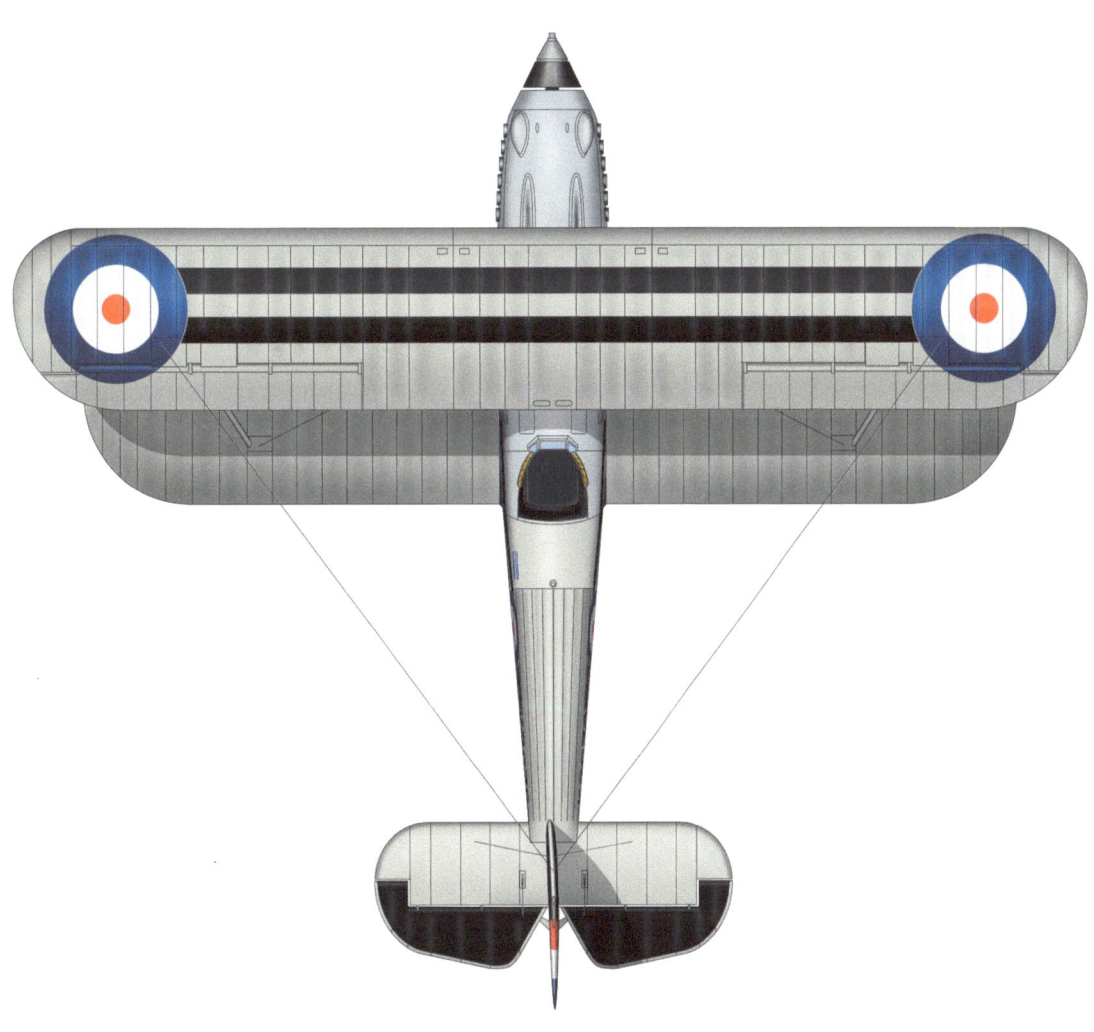

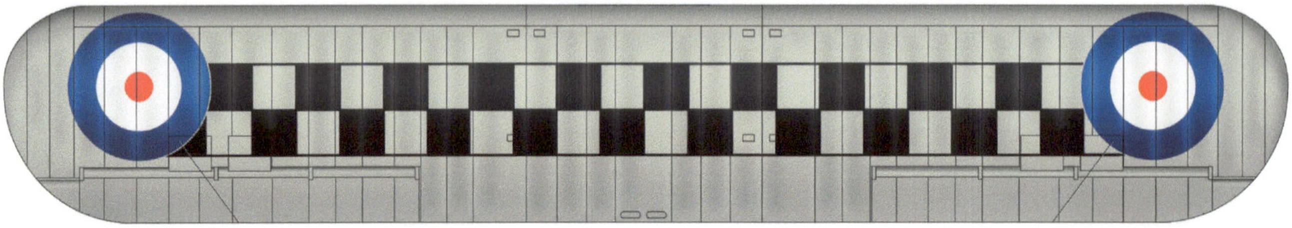

Hawker Fury Mk.I K3731, No.43 Squadron, Tangmere, 1936.
Note the squadron badge on the fin. The painted fin and tailplane denotes A Flight Commander's mount. In most cases, the white checks of No.43 Squadron markings were not painted.
(see p 26)

Right : On the early years of service with No.43 Squadron, the Squadron Commander was flying K1930 with this specific marking on the tail, with black checks painted on the fin and elevators.

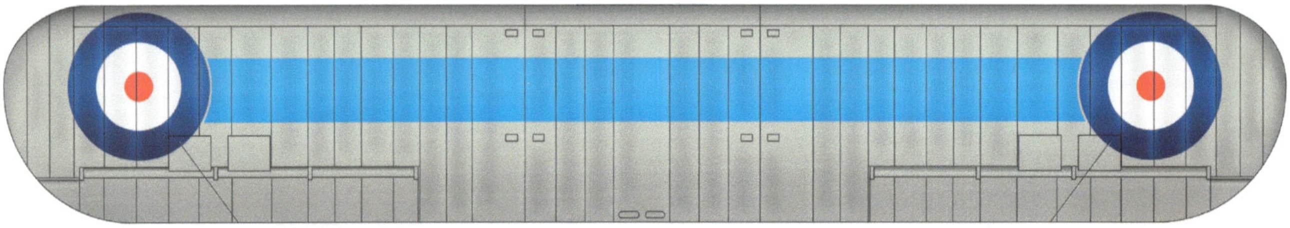

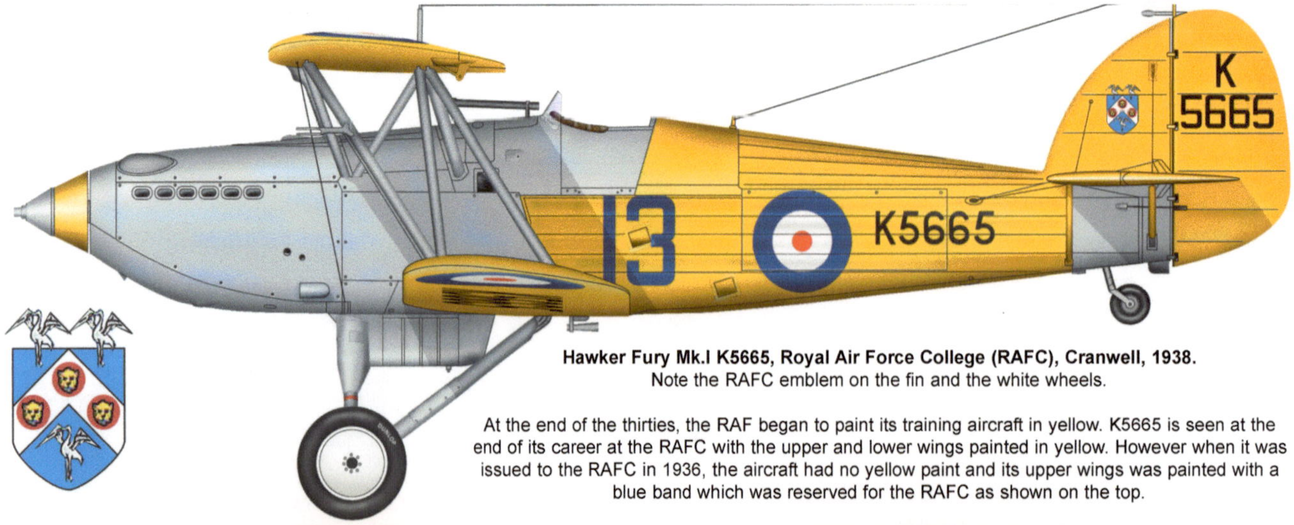

Hawker Fury Mk.I K5665, Royal Air Force College (RAFC), Cranwell, 1938.
Note the RAFC emblem on the fin and the white wheels.

At the end of the thirties, the RAF began to paint its training aircraft in yellow. K5665 is seen at the end of its career at the RAFC with the upper and lower wings painted in yellow. However when it was issued to the RAFC in 1936, the aircraft had no yellow paint and its upper wings was painted with a blue band which was reserved for the RAFC as shown on the top.

Up to the end of the thirties, all RAF aircraft had the serial painted under the wings in opposite position to be easily readable from below.

The SAAF
April 1936 - June 1943

Bridge on 20 June 1938. Some also saw service with the Central Flying School at Upavon, 1 Air Armament School for use in gunnery training and 2 Anti-Aircraft Co-operation Unit. Many other aircraft were used as ground instructional airframes in the Technical Training Schools after accident or after they have reached their airframe limit.

The Royal Air Force College at Cranwell had a number of Furies on strength with its Advanced Training Flight. The first four, K5678 and K5680-K5682, were delivered on 12 December 1935. In all five were used by the RAFC, all but one being totally new, coming straight from the factory or a Aircraft Storage Unit. On the 7 October 1936 Flight Lieutenant Roy J.O. Bartlett, K5682, and Flight Cadet Howard F. Burton, K5681, were up practising gun camera attacks when the aircraft collided. Both pilots baled out of their aircraft but the parachute of Flight Lieutenant Bartlett got tangled up in the tail of his Fury and he was carried to his death.

By the outbreak of war, only 35 of 118 Furies Mk.I were still in the RAF inventory. They continued to soldier on for a couple of month as advanced trainer, a task which ended early in July 1940. They were sent for storage, but a handful of them, which had not reached their airframe limit, were sold to the SAAF in the following weeks where they had the opportunity to be engaged in action, opening a new chapter to the Fury history.

The connection with the Hawker Fury in South Africa began with the South African Minister of Defence, the Honourable Mr Oswald Piron K.C., who introduced a five-year expansion plan for the South African Air Force (SAAF) in 1934. Two years later a decision was made to purchase the Hawker Fury as South Africa' s front line fighter. Seven Hawker Fury aircraft built by General Aircraft Ltd were ordered in 1936 which were based on the RAF Fury Mk.II (to be developed in a future Allied Wings) with the Kestrel VI engine but fitted with Browning machine guns instead of Vickers. They were allotted serial numbers 200 to 206. The first six arrived at Cape Town on the *City of Nagpur* on 24 April 1936 and following assembly and test flights were flown to Pretoria via Port Elizabeth, where they took part in a display to commemorate the opening of the new city airport. They were initially issued to 'C' Flight of the Central Flying School, and in September transferred to 'G' Flight. On 14 December 1938, the SAAF lost its first Fury when during an aerobatic display at Voortrekker Monument, Fury 201 crashed, its pilot, Lieutenant St.E. Truter being safe.

A few days later, four Furies were issued to No.3 (Comms) Squadron for a short period and on 5 September 1939 they were sent to No.4 (Fighter) Squadron in Durban. Trouble with the Kestrel engine bearings forced a temporary grounding of the Furies. This unit was re-designated No.2 Squadron on 1 December but in April 1940 they were sent to the Reserve Aircraft Park (RAP). Six were eventually issued to No.1 Squadron, SAAF in June 1940 for subsequent use in East Africa since Italy had entered into war on 10 June 1940.

Meanwhile, with the outbreak of WWII the defence of South Africa rested on the shoulders of a few obsolete Furies and a handful of newly acquired Hurricanes so the SAAF decided to purchase some other fighters. In December 1939, 22 Hawker Furies and 28 Gloster Gauntlets were ordered as part of a large package while the RAF decided to transfer 18 Gladiators to reinforce the SAAF fighter forces. The Gauntlet order was cancelled at the request of the Air Ministry and 24 Gauntlets were diverted to Finland, the remaining four were eventually purchased by South Africa in May 1940. All the Furies were former RAF Mk.I for which was remaining airframe hours. They were

Fury 202 at the time it was serving at the Central Flying School before the war. It will later be involved in an air collision with Fury 204 in August 1940 and was destroyed. (*SAAF Museum*)

Fury 208 in East Africa in 1940. Except the national markings and serial nothing else is painted on this Fury. (*SAAF Museum*)

delivered in four batches between August and November 1940. Immediately after they arrival at Durban in the *Buteshiere* on 10 August 1940, the first batch of six Furies serialled 207 to 212 were re-shipped to Mombasa on the 15 on board of the "Kato" to reinforce No.1 Squadron.

INTO ACTION

The first taste of action for the Furies occurred on the 3 August 1940 when three aircraft were scrambled after a lone Caproni Ca133 from 8a Squadriglia, 25° *Gruppo* was seen approaching the base. One of the Furies (206 piloted by Lieutenant Pannell) failed to start but the other two pursued the Caproni. Closing in on the enemy aircraft Lieutenant Rushmere in 205 fired off a burst before both his guns jarmmed. Flight Lieutenant R.S. Blake in Fury 203 then took over and carried out a number of head on attacks. After firing a long burst into the cockpit the Caproni attempted to land but crashed and burst into flames about 7 miles from Wajir. It was thought that Lieutenant Rushmere had fired the critical burst before his guns jarmmed and therefore both pilots received joint credit for the destruction of the Caproni.

The next day two Furies flown by Lieutenant B.R. Dimmock in Fury 202 and Lieutenant G.L. McBride in Fury 204 collided over Nanyuki. Both pilots were able to bale out with minor injuries It was the third loss suffered by No.1 Squadron as previously, on the 12 July Lieutenant J.D. Niblock-Stuart's Fury (200) had suffered engine trouble and had to carry out a forced landing at Mukogodo. Although the undercarriage was damaged during the landing the Fury was later flown out and repaired. Two days later, on the 6th, a formation of Ca133s was intercepted near Wajir by two Furies. Both pilots concentrated on one of the bombers and managed to knock out the centre engine before it escaped into cloud. On the following day Lieutenant Burger was sent after a lone Ca133 to the North of Wajir. To his disappointment he was unable to catch the faster aircraft. In early September Lieutenant Rushmere overshot his landing while on his way to Wajir and hit a bush. The fabric was torn from the lower starboard wing of his Fury and one blade of the propeller lost the tip. Both blades were cut back by 4" to enable Rushmere to continue with his journey. On the 11th Rushmere overturned his Fury when he ran into a filled-in bomb crater.

Their stay with No.1 Squadron was short lived however as all the remaining Furies were transferred to No.2 Squadron (which was also equipped with five Hurricanes and nine Gladiators) on 1 October 1940 which then could count on nine Furies, a number soon reduced to eight when Fury 206 crashed during a mock attack on Hawker Hartbees at Wajir on 5 October. Its pilot, Lieutenant D.C. Uys was severely injured. They were joined by the batch of six Furies (223 to 228) which had arrived at Durban on 20 October 1940 with the *Clan Mathieson* and were put into No.2 Squadron inventory in January 1941. These were scattered about the airfields at Nairobi, Mombasa, Nanyuki, Archers Post, Garissa, Ndeges Nest and Wajir. Due to the searing heat the Furies were plagued with overheating engines. Additional slots were cut into the engine cowling to provide more air for cooling. The tropical conditions also affected the Fury's performance. As a result it was intended that they would only be used for close support and as escorts for the Hartbeeste two seat bombers. With a severe shortage of fighters the Furies would be pressed more and more into the fighter role, for which it was now totally inadequate. On 19 October three Ca133s raided Garissa. Furies of 'F' Detachment were scrambled to intercept.

Three No.2 Squadron Furies starting up and taxying out at Husseini, Kenya in early 1941. (*via Michael Schoeman*)

Lieutenant Hendrik Burger in Fury 200 was able to catch one of the bombers and after a number of passes it carried out a forced landing. Lieutenant Wiese attacked another bomber and hit it with a long burst before losing it in the gathering darkness. Two days later the Furies were again scrambled but failed to catch the faster bombers.

On the last day of the month a number of senior officers were on a tour of the area when there was a near disaster. Two SAAF Ju86s approached Archers Post. On board were Major General Cunningham, General Smuts, Major General Goodwin-Austen, General van Ryneveld and the AOC, Air Commodore Sowrey. The Junkers were escorted by two Hurricanes. No one had informed those at Archers Post about the incoming aircraft, and therefore three Furies were scrambled to intercept the unidentified aircraft. As Captain Jack Meaker closed in on the lead aircraft he noticed it had twin rudders. All Italian aircraft encountered so far had a single fin and rudder. Pulling up he then noticed the SAAF roundels on the wings and recognised it as a Junkers Ju86. With no radio he could not alert his colleagues and could only watch in horror as one Fury went in to attack. Lieutenant Pannell bored into attack and fired a burst at one of the Junkers. The pilot dived away to port and under the other Ju86, which took the full force of Pannells attack as he followed the lead Junkers. It was only when he broke away that Pannell realised that he had fired on a South African aircraft. The Junkers suffered damage in the wing root but thankfully nobody on board was injured. By the end of December No.2 Squadron had 9 Furies still on strength, although most were in poor condition. In February the squadron had to give up its remaining three Hurricanes to No.1 Squadron. In return they received further Furies to bring their complement up to 12. On 9 February 1941 two Furies were detached to Wajir, with a further two, arriving later the next day. A number of patrols were carried out on the 10th but these proved to be uneventful. On the 14th Captain Meaker had a hair-raising flight in Fury 213. He was up on patrol when the two port wing spars snapped just outboard of the struts. Regaining control he was able to land and the ground crew set about repairing the damage. Later that day the repairs had been completed with (among other things) some water piping and petrol tins. Captain Meaker took it up for an air test, which included aerobatics and stalls, and pronounced it satisfactory. The next day it was flown down to Garissa for a new port wing. The Furies continued with fighter and escort duties but they were by now totally worn out.

In April 1941 they were again transferred to No.4 Squadron at Nanyuki, Kenya, for training. With the departure of No.4 Squadron to Egypt in May, they were handed over to No.70 OTU at Nakuru and eleven were shipped back to the Union in March 1942 to serve with other SAAF squadrons.

AT HOME

At home, No .13 Squadron at Swartkop received six Furies (213 to 218) in January 1941. This batch had been delivered to Durban on 20 October 1940 with the *Clan Mathieso*. Soon after No.13 Squadron was renumbered as No.43 Squadron. They were joined by the last four Furies which arrived on 7

Line up of Furies of No.70 OTU at Nakuru, Kenya during the summer of 1941. Fury 205 is on the front. (*via Andrew Thomas*)

Claim list of SAAF Furies

Date	Pilot	Origin	S/N	A/c flown	Type	Conf.	Prob.
03.08.40	F/L Robert S. **Blake**	(SA)/RAF	RAF No.37274	203	Ca133	0.5	-
	Lt Patrick K.Q. **Rushmere**	SAAF	SAAF No.44149V	205	Ca133	0.5	-
19.10.40	Lt Hendrik J.P. **Burger**	SAAF	SAAF No.103205V	200	Ca133	1.0	-

Total:
2 aircraft destroyed,
1 damaged.

Above:
Four No.2 Squadron pilots are standing in front of a Hawker Fury, end 1940. From left to right, Walter P. Stanford, Frank J. Meaker, J.A. "Japie" Wiese and Patrck K.Q. Rushmere who claimed a shared victory with Flight Lieutenant R.S. Blake. All survived the war. *(via Andrew Thomas)*

Above:
Robert S. Blake was a South African from Pretoria who joined the RAF on a short service commission in September 1935 and was as a Flight Lieutenant with No.54 Squadron. Granting special leave in South Africa in Spring 1940, he accompanied No.1 Squadron in Kenya when Italy entered the war and claimed the second victory of the SAAF in August sharing it with Ptarick Rushmere. Later founder member of No.2 Squadron, he would claim a confirmed victiry in board of an Hurricane the following 25 October. He was shot down four days later to become a PoW until East Africa fell to Commonwealth forces and his wounds sustained that day kept him away from any operational postings until the end of the war.
(Michael Schoeman)

Right:
Even of poor quality, this is a rare photograph of a Fury from No.1 Sqn taken during an operational patrol.
(via Andrew Thomas)

SAAF Furies Aircraft History

Seven Hawker Fury to Contract 361724/34 delivered to Cape Town (CT)

200	Del CT 22.05.36; CFS Feb.37; 3 Sqn 19.12.38; Waterkloof 30.08.39; 4 Sqn 05.09.39; 2 Sqn 01.12.39; RAP 05.04.40; Durban 24.05.40; 1 Sqn 23.06.40; 2 Sqn 01.10.40; 4 Sqn 14.04.41; 6 AD 07.07.41 for repair; 105 MU 21.07.41; Durban Feb.42; 43 Sqn 28.05.42; 6 Sqn 29.08.42; 2 AD 03.05 43; Bos 18.05.43; Soc 06.01.44 - (TT 346h45)
201	Del CT 24.04.36; CFS 26.05.36; Crashed during aerobatic display at Voortrekker Monument 14.12.38; Soc 24.06.39.
202	Del CT 24.04.36; CFS 26.05.36; 3 Sqn 19.12.38; RAP 22.03.39; HQ 24.06.39; 4 Sqn 05.09.39; 2 Sqn 01.12.39; RAP 05.04.40 ;Durban 23.05.40; 1 Sqn 23.06.40; Collided with Fury 204 during mock attack Nanyuki 04.08.40.
203	Del CT 24.04.36; CFS 26.05.36; 3 Sqn 19.12.38; RAP 22.03.39 Waterkloof 30.08.39; 4 Sqn 05.09.39; 2 Sqn 01.12.39; RAP 0504.40; Durban 23.05.40; 1 Sqn 23.06.40; 2 Sqn 01.10.40; 4 Sqn 14.04.41; 6 AD 21.06.41; Durban Feb.42; 1 AD Mar.42; 6 Sqn 04.09.42; Force landed at Beaufort West in bad weather 09.10.42; 2 AD; 43 Sqn; 2 AD 10.01.44; Soc 22.05.44 - (TT 410h45)
204	Del CT 24.04.36; CFS 26.05.36; RAP .38;HQ 24.06.39; 4 Sqn 05.09.39; 2 Sqn 01.12.39; RAP 05.04.40; Durban 24.05.40; 1 Sqn 23.06.40; Collided with Fury 202 during mock attack Nanyuki 04.08.40.
205	Del CT 24.04.36; CFS 26.05.36; 3 Sqn 19.12.38; RAP 22.03.39; Waterkloof 30.08.39; 4 Sqn 05.09.39; 2 Sqn 01.12.39; RAP 05.04.40; Durban 21.05.40; 1 Sqn 23.06.40; 2 Sqn 01.10.40; 4 Sqn 14.04.41; 70 OTU May 41; Durban Feb.42; 1 AD Mar.42; 43 Sqn 07.07.42; 6 Sqn 02.09.42; Crashed in Paardeberg Mts 12.01.43; Bos 05.02.43; Soc 14.06.43.
206	Del CT 24.04.36; CFS 26.05.36; RAP 38; HQ 24.06.39; 2 Sqn 04.09.39; 2 Sqn 01.12.39; Durban 23.05.40; 1 Sqn 23.06.40; Crashed in high speed stall in mock attack on Hartbees at Wajir 05.10.40; Soc 21.10.40.

Fury 206 of the original batch in flight in 1936. *(SAAF Museum)*

Six Hawker Fury delivered to Durban 10.08.40 with 'Buteshire' Re-shipped to Mombasa 15.08.40 with 'Kato'

207	**ex-K5663**; 1 Sqn 28.08.40; 2 Sqn 01.10.40 ?; 4 Sqn 14.04.41; 70 OTU May 41; Durban Feb.42; 1AD 42; 43 Sqn Jun.42; 6 Sqn 04.09.42; 2 AD 28.07.43; Bos 21.09.43; Soc 06.01.44 - (TT 746h)
208	**ex-K3733**; 1 Sqn 28.08.40; 2 Sqn 01.10.40; 6 AD 21.05.41 after crash; Durban Feb.42; 1 AD Mar.42; 43 Sqn 12.05.42; Stalled and crashed in mock attack at Cato Ridge 06.07.42; Soc 12.09.42 - (TT 457h30)
209	**ex-K3735**; 1 Sqn 28.08.40; 2 Sqn 01.10.40; 4 Sqn 14.04.41; 70 OTU May 41; Durban Feb.42; 1AD Mar.42; 43 Sqn 05.06.42 Engine failure, overturned in force landing at Roodekop 19.06.42; 1 AD; Bos 09.09.42; Soc 01.12.42. - (TT 704h25)
210	**ex-K5669**; 1 Sqn 28.08.40; 2 Sqn 01.10.40; 4 Sqn 14.04.41; 70 OTU MAy 41; Durban Feb.42; 1 AD Mar.42; 43 Sqn 28.04.42; 6 Sqn 02.09.42; Stalled in mock attack on A-A post 12.01.43; Bos 05.02.43; Soc 14.06.43. - (TT 738h10)
211	**ex-K 5672**; 1 Sqn 28.08.40; 2 Sqn 01.10.40; 4 Sqn 14.04.41; 70 OTU May.41; Durban Feb.42; 1 AD Mar.42; 43 Sqn 28.05.42; 6 Sqn 04.09.42; 2 AD 28.07.43; 69 AS 24.08.44; Bos; Soc 1944. - (TT 695h50) To SA War Museum 07.07.44; Scrapped 1951?

| 212 | ex-K5670; 1 Sqn 28.08.40; 2 Sqn 01.10.40; 4 Sqn 14.04.41; 70 OTU May 41; Durban Feb.42; 1 AD Mar.42; 43 Sqn 12.06.42, **coded Y?**; 6 Sqn 29.08.42; Brake failure on landing, swung and overturned at Eerste Rivier 02.05.43; 2 AD; Bos 04.11.43; Soc 06.01.44. - (TT 733h20) |

Note : On 24.12.40 Lt Niblock-Stuart killed in cr of Fury 5663 at Archer's Post.

With no wings and propeller, what we believe to 212 is lying in very poor condition.
(Stefaan Bouwer)

Six Hawker Fury delivered to Durban 20.10.40 with 'Clan Mathieso'

213	ex-?; 23 AS 15.11.40; 1 AD 12.12.40; 43 Sqn Oct.41, **coded J**; 6 Sqn 04.09.42; Swung on landing; overturned at Eerste Rivier 16.04.43; Cat 2; Soc 2 AD 25.10.43 - (TT 988h10)
214	ex-K5678; 13 Sqn; 43 Sqn 41; 6 Sqn 04.09.42; Tyre burst on landing, badly damaged 25.03.43; 2 AD 03.04.43; 43 Sqn; 2 AD 10.01.44; Soc 13.07.44. (TT - 769h50)
215	ex-K5674; 23 AS 15.11.40; 1 AD 12.12.40; 13 Sqn 15.03.41; Ran out of fuel and force landed near Pitsani 31.03.41; Cat 2: 70 AS for Instruction 15.04.41; 73 AS 13.09.43; 1 AD 15.08.44; Bos; Soc 13.07.44 - (TT403h40). Being restored in UK.
216	ex-?; 4 AD 28.10.40; 23 AS 15.11.40; 13 Sqn 12.12.40; 43 Sqn May 41, **coded L**; 6 Sqn 04.09.42; 43 Sqn; 2 AD 10.01.44; Bos 07.03.44? Soc 22.05.44. - (TT 1,003h10)
217	ex-K1979; 4 AD 28.10.40; 13 Sqn 03.12.40; 43 Sqn 08.08.41 **coded M**; 6 Sqn 29.08.42; 2 AD 09.12.42; Bos 03.11.43; Soc 06.01.44. (TT 1,059h40)
218	ex-K2050; 4 AD 28.10.40; 13 Sqn; 43 Sqn May 41 **coded N**; 1 AD Aug.41; 43 Sqn 18.02.42; 6 Sqn 04.09.42; 2 AD 29.06.43; Bos 23.08.43; Soc 06.01.44. - (TT 885h35)

Four Hawker Fury delivered to Durban 07.11.40 with 'Australia Star'

219	ex-?; 4 AD 18.11.40; 43 Sqn Apr.41; 1 AD 20.02.42; 43 Sqn 24.03 .42; 6 Sqn 04.09.42; 2 AD; Soc 06.01.44.(TT 853h30)
220	ex-K5680; 4 AD 16.11.40; 43 Sqn Apr.41; 6 Sqn 04.09.42; 43 Sqn ; 2 AD 10.01.44; Soc 22.05.44. - (TT 713h20)
221	ex-?; 4 AD 16.11.40; 43 Sqn Apr.41; Crashed at Zwartkop 03.08.41 - NFD; Soc 30.03.42.
222	ex-K2899; 4 AD 18.11.40;13 Sqn Apr.41; Force landed at Mafeking 02.04.41; 69 AS 07.04.41 for instruction as No.IS 51; Soc 11.09.44. (TT 812h)

Six Hawker Fury delivered to Durban 20.10.40 with 'Clan Mathieson'; Re-shipped to Mombasa 28.10.40 or 28 11 40.

223	ex-K2877; 2 SqnJan.41; 4 Sqn Apr.41; 6 AD May 41; Durban Feb.42; 1 AD Mar.42; 43 Sqn 28.04.42; 6 Sqn 04.09.42; Stalled on landing, hit wind break and overturned at Eerste Rivier 19.05 .43; Soc Nov.43 - (TT 631h20)
224	ex-K2071; 2 Sqn Jan.41; NFD
225	ex-K3741; 2 Sqn Jan.41; 4 Sqn 14.04.41; 70 OTU May 41; Durban Feb.42; 1 AD Mar.42; 43 Sqn May.42; 6 Sqn 04.09.42; 2 AD 01.03.43; 43 Sqn Aug.43; Swung on landing at Barberton 27.09.43; 2 AD 07.01.44 ; Soc 13.07.44 - (TT 652h40)
226	ex-K5676; 2 Sqn Jan.41; 4 Sqn; Crashed 28.06.41 - NFD; To ARS 06.07.41; Soc 17.09.41 - (TT 683h30)
227	ex-K3740; 2 Sqn Jan.41; NFD.
228	ex-K5675; 2 Sqn Jan.4; 4 Sqn 14.04.41; 70 OTU May 41; Durban Feb.42; 1 AD Mar.42; 43 Sqn 15.04.42; 6 Sqn 04.09.42; crashed ? 11.12.42?; 2 AD 21.09.43; Bos 19.10.43; Soc 06.01.44 - (TT 714h30)

Note; There are no official records of Fury aircraft nos 223 to 228 operating in East Africa; Pilot's log books and official documents however refer to Fury aircraft nos 213 to 218 in East Africa;
One can assume that on arrival, these six aircraft were numbered onwards from nos 208 to 212 which were already in EA and that the signal allotting the number listed above was not received in time.

Aircraft Lost by Accident
SAAF

Date	Unit	Pilot	SN	Origin	Serial	Fate
14.12.38	CFS	Lt St.Elmo Truter	SAAF No.P102610V	SAAF	201	-
04.08.40	1 Sqn	Lt Bernard R. Dimmock	SAAF No.47412V	SAAF	202	-
	1 Sqn	Lt Gilbert L. McBride	SAAF No.102859V	SAAF	204	-
05.10.40	1 Sqn	Lt Dirk C. Uys	SAAF No.47434V	SAAF	206	-
24.12.40	2 Sqn	Lt John D. Niblock-Stuart*	SAAF No.47700V	SAAF	(207)	†
31.03.41	13 Sqn	2/Lt Peter M. Hedley	SAAF No.103079V	SAAF	215	-
02.04.41	13 Sqn	2/Lt George F. Raubenheimer	SAAF No.103387	SAAF	222	-
28.06.41	4 Sqn	No details available	?	?	226	-
03.08.41	43 Sqn	No details available	?	?	221	-
19.06.42	43 Sqn	Lt Jacob A.K. D'Alebout	SAAF No.47830V	SAAF	209	-
06.07.42	43 Sqn	2/Lt Marthinus J. Krugel	SAAF No.205992	SAAF	208	†
12.01.43	6 Sqn	Lt Archibald McCurdy	SAAF No.103626	SAAF	210	†
14.01.43	6 Sqn	Lt Derek H. de L'Ange	SAAF No.205732	SAAF	205	†
16.04.43	6 Sqn	Lt Maurice J.W. Palmer	SAAF No.205871V	SAAF	213	-
02.05.43	6 Sqn	Lt Aidan C. Riley	SAAF No.236569	SAAF	212	-
19.05.43	6 Sqn	Lt Charles A.D. Williams	SAAF No.41334V	SAAF	223	-

*Lt Niblock-Stuart was killed in Fury K5663, meaning that the SAAF serial was not painted yet at the time of his death. The aircraft was repaired.

Total: 15

Left:
If the name of the No.4 Squadron's pilot who wrecked Fury 226 on 28 June 1941 remains unknown, the results of his action were taken by the camera. More generally speaking if the SAAF lost more than half of its Fury fleet over the years, which is a pretty high loss ratio, it must be noticed only four pilots were killed and none in action.
(via Andrew Thomas)

Fury 213/J of No.43 Squadron in 1942 waiting for its pilot as doing the mechanic, lying on the grass.
It was later destroyed in accident in April 1943.
(Stefaan Bouwer)

COMBINED ROLL OF HONOUR
RAF (FURY MK.I)
AND **SAAF**

Name	Rank	Age	Origin	Date	Serial
ASHTON, Norman Dorrington	P/O	21	RAF	27.06.35	K3742
BARTLETT, Roy James Oliphant	F/L	31	RAF	07.10.36	K5682
BAXTER, Matthew Henry	Sgt	25	RAF	04.04.38	K2074
BAXTER, Merton Vivian	P/O	22	(NZ)/RAF	22.02.38	K2061
BROWN, Richard	F/L	n/k	RAF	23.04.34	K2047
FERRIS, Albert Edward Ralph	P/O	27	RAF	02.08.37	K5666
HODGE, William Molesworth	Sgt	n/k	RAF	25.09.33	K2073
JACKSON, Neville Howard	P/O	20	RAF	26.05.32	K2064
HOLLINGS, George Edmund	P/O	n/k	RAF	30.10.36	K1941
KRUGEL, Marthinus Jacobus	2/Lt	n/k	SAAF	06.07.42	208[1]
de L'ANGE, Derek Hugo	Lt	20	SAAF	14.01.43	205
McCURDY, Archibald	Lt	20	SAAF	12.01.43	210[3]
MILBURN, Colin William Edward	P/O	n/k	RAF	20.06.38	K3730
NIBLOCK-STUART, John Douglas	Lt	23	SAAF	24.12.40	K5663[2]
PATTEN, Robert Edmund	Sgt	n/k	RAF	17.12.37	K2901
PECK, Harry Hamilton	P/O	n/k	RAF	17.12.37	K2902
ROLPH, Robert Vincent	P/O	20	(CAN)/RAF	28.02.33	K1936
TANFIELD, John Geoffrey	Sgt	n/k	RAF	29.05.37	K2076
TANNER, William Erskrine Snell	F/O	n/k	RAF	23.04.34	K2044

Total:

RAF: 15
(including 1 Canadian and 1 New-Zealander)
SAAF: 4

n/k : not known

1: Serial K3733 for the RAF
2: The aircraft was repaired. Serial 207 for the SAAF. SAAF serial not painted yet when the accident occured.
3: Serial K5669 for the RAF

Hawker Fury Mk.I 213/J, No.43 Squadron, SAAF, Zwartkop, South Africa, end 1941.
Below top view of 213.

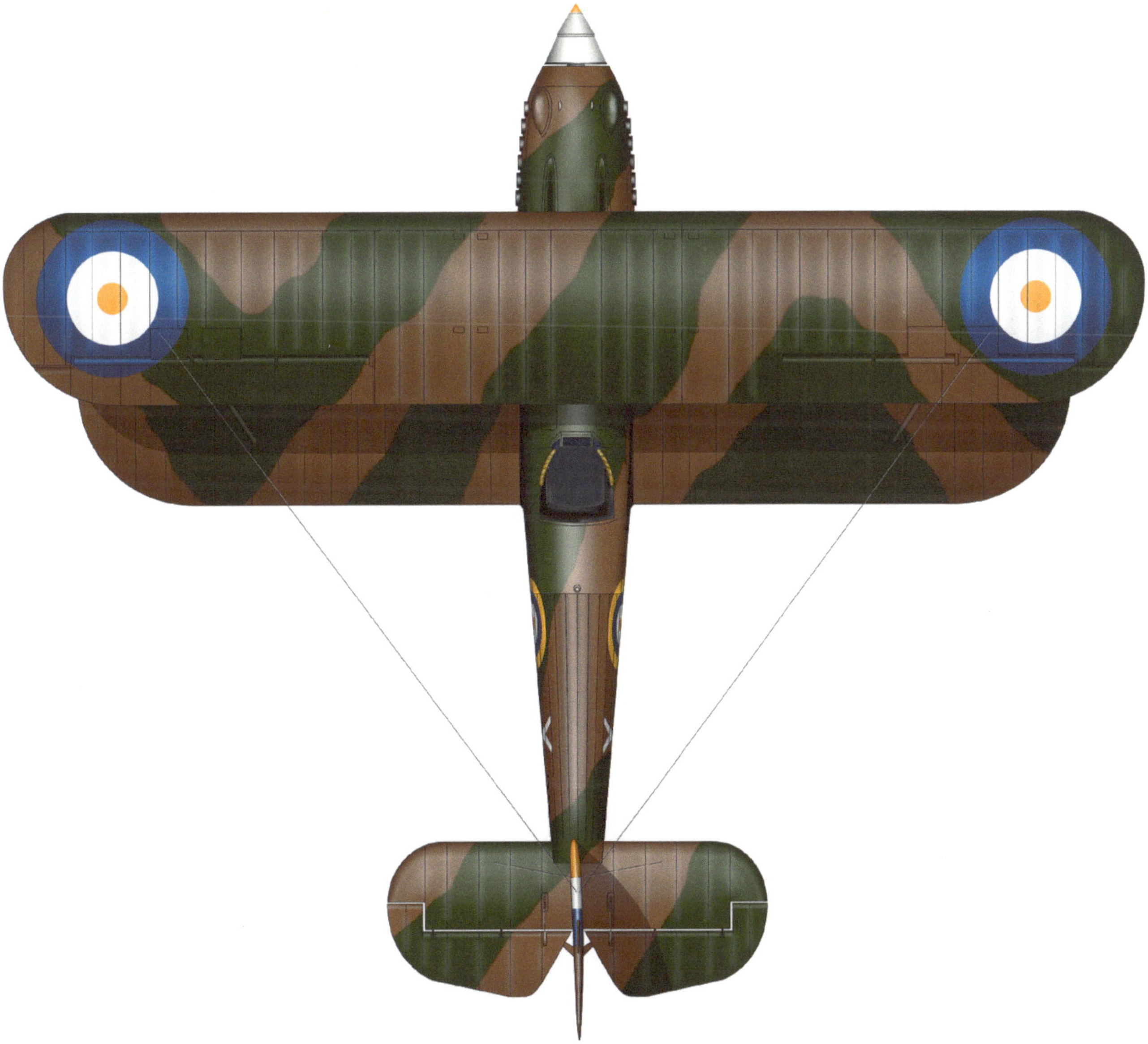

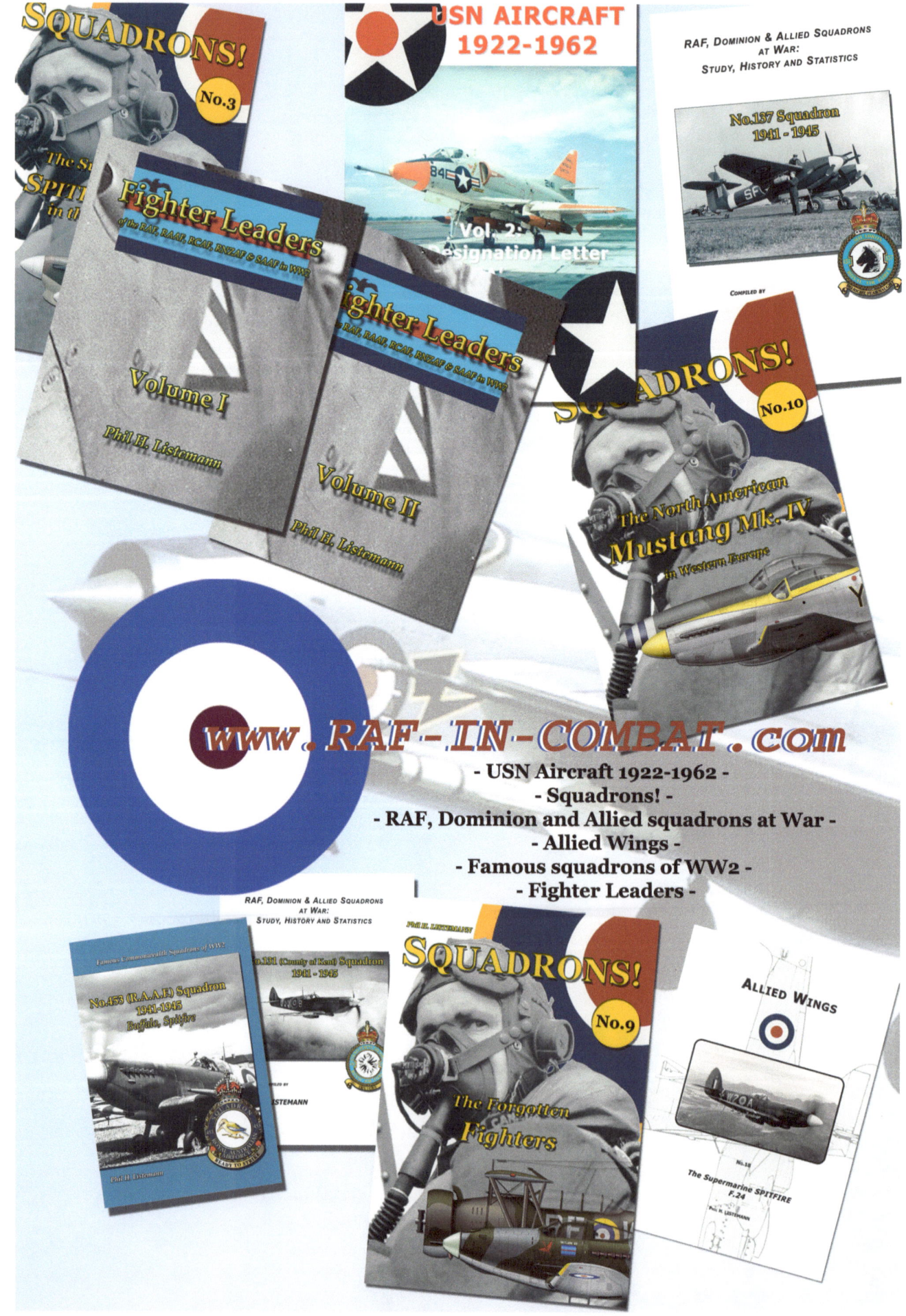

www.ingramcontent.com/pod-product-compliance
Lightning Source LLC
Chambersburg PA
CBHW060759090426
42736CB00002B/82